God's Words to My Heart

By

Greg Hadley

Booksurge.com

Copyright © 2008 by Greg Hadley

All rights reserved. No part of this book may be reproduced, scanned or distributed in any printed or electronic form without permission. Please do not participate or encourage piracy of copyrighted materials in violation of the author's rights. Purchase only authorized editions.

Biblical texts are taken from the New American Bible, published by Catholic Bible Press, a division of Thomas Nelson Publishers, Nashville, Tennessee.

Hadley, Greg [1934—]
 God's Words to My Heart / Greg Hadley —1st ed.

ISBN: 1-4392-2142-1

Printed in the United States of America
10 9 8 7 6 5 4 3 2 1

*We understand the words of God more truly
when we search out ourselves in them.*

St. Gregory the Great

TABLE OF CONTENTS
BY PAGE

FOREWORD i
PREFACE iii
ACKNOWLEDGEMENTS vi
ADORATION 1

    John 3:16 1
    Genesis 1:31a 1
    Mark 12:28-31 2
    Luke 16:13 3
    John 1:38–39 4
    John 3:36 and 5:24 5
    John 6:44 6
    Romans 11:33 7
    Romans 13:9–10 8
    Psalm 9:2–3 9
    Philippians 2:10–11 9
    1 Thessalonians 5:9 10
    2 Thessalonians 2:3 11
    Hebrews 11:3 11
    James 2:14, 16, 26 12
    2 Peter 3:18 13
    Genesis 3:19b 14
    Mark 14:36 14
    Numbers 6:24–26 15
    Luke 12:8 16
    Luke 24:13–35 16
    John 15:16a 18
    Romans 6:8 18
    Romans 8:15 19
    1 Corinthians 2:9 20
    Psalm 23:1–6 20
    2 Corinthians 3:5 21

2 Corinthians 10:18	21
James 1:22	22
Ecclesiastes 3:1–8	23
Matthew 5:16	23
Matthew 13:1–9	24
Matthew 18:20	25
Matthew 20:26–28	26
Matthew 26:26–28	27
Matthew 28:19	28
Genesis 9:13	29
Mark 14:61–62	29
Luke 10:2	30
John 1:14	31
John 6:35, 51	32
Romans 2:16	33
Romans 8:18	34
1 Corinthians 15:55	34
2 Corinthians 3:17	35
Philippians 3:20	36
Colossians 3:2	36
2 Timothy 3:16	37
Hebrews 13:2	38
Revelation 3:16	39
Romans 8:26–27	40
John 21:25	40
CONTRITION	**42**
Matthew 3:1–2	42
Matthew 6:20–21	43
Matthew 12:30	43
Matthew 18:21–22	44
Matthew 26:39	45
Mark 9:41	45
Luke 6:37	46
Luke 23:34	47
Acts 2:32	47
Acts 15:22	48

Romans 7:19	49
Ephesians 5:25	49
Colossians 3:13–14	50
Matthew 19:23 and Luke 18:24–25	51
Matthew 25:31–46	52
Matthew 27:46	54
Luke 6:27–28	55
Luke 6:41	55
Luke 15:7	56
Acts 3:19	57
Acts 17:30	57
Romans 12:4–5	58
Proverbs 13:3	59
Philippians 2:14	60
Colossians 2:8	60
1 Timothy 1:14b	61
Hebrews 12:7	62
1 Peter 1:24–25	62
1 John 2:3	63
Matthew 11:28–30	64
Deuteronomy 4:2	65
Luke 6:31	65
Luke 12:15	66
Luke 15:11–32	67
Acts 2:28	68
Acts 7:60	69
Romans 6:23	69
Tobit 3:3	70
1 Thessalonians 4:13	71
1 Thessalonians 5:22	72
James 2:13	72
1 Peter 5:8	73

THANKSGIVING **75**

Matthew 25:29	75
Luke 4:13	76
Luke 12:6–7	76

Romans 5:19 77
2 Samuel 22:28–29 78
2 Corinthians 9:6–7b 78
Galatians 5:22–23 79
Psalm 91:10–12 80
Proverbs 18:22 81
Matthew 5:1–12 81
Matthew 10:19–20 83
Matthew 16:18–19 83
Luke 17:17–18 85
1 Chronicles 16:34 86
1 Corinthians 15:22–23 86
Colossians 3:17 87
1 Thessalonians 5:16–18 87
Revelation 1:19 88
Matthew 24:35–36, 44 89
Mark 9:37 90
Luke 21:1–4 91
1 Corinthians 12:4–6 92
Galatians 3:28 93
Proverbs 17:6 93
1 John 2:15 94
Luke 12:48 95

SUPPLICATION 96

Matthew 7:21 96
Matthew 16:24–26 97
Matthew 21:22 98
Mark 6:50b 98
Exodus 3:11 99
Luke 12:22–24 100
Luke 12:34 100
1 Corinthians 9:24 101
1 Corinthians 13:1, 13 102
1 Corinthians 16:13 102
Philippians 4:6–7 103
2 Timothy 1:7 104

Hebrews 13:6 104
3 John 1:4 105
Isaiah 55:8–9 106
Matthew 7:7–8 107
Matthew 23:12 and Luke 13:30 107
Mark 7:21–23 108
Mark 10:51 109
1 Corinthians 10:13 110
Galatians 6:9 110
Ephesians 6:13 111
2 Timothy 3:12 112
Mark 11:24 113
Romans 12:18 114
1 Corinthians 3:16 114
Psalm 71:9 115
Ephesians 2:8 116
1 Timothy 5:17 116
Sirach (Ecclesiasticus) 3:12–14a 117
Isaiah 55:10–11 118
2 Maccabees 15 (Epilogue):37 (parts) 119

ENDNOTES 120
AFTERWORD 126
ABOUT THE AUTHOR 127

TABLE OF CONTENTS
BY BIBLICAL ORDER

Genesis 1:31a 1
Genesis 3:19b 14
Genesis 9:13 29
Exodus 3:11 99
Numbers 6:24–26 15
Deuteronomy 4:2 65
2 Samuel 22:28–29 78
1 Chronicles 16:34 86
Tobit 3:3 70
2 Maccabees 15 (Epilogue):37 (parts) 119
Psalm 9:2–3 9
Psalm 23:1–6 20
Psalm 71:9 115
Psalm 91:10–12 80
Proverbs 13:3 59
Proverbs 17:6 93
Proverbs 18:22 81
Ecclesiastes 3:1–8 23
Sirach (Ecclesiasticus) 3:12–14a 117
Isaiah 55:8–9 106
Isaiah 55:10–11 118

ଈଈ

Matthew 3:1–2 42
Matthew 5:1–12 81
Matthew 5:16 23
Matthew 6:20–21 43
Matthew 7:7–8 107
Matthew 7:21 96
Matthew 10:19–20 117
Matthew 11:28–30 64
Matthew 12:30 43
Matthew 13:1–9 24
Matthew 16:18–19 83

Matthew 16:24–26	97
Matthew 18:20	25
Matthew 18:21–22	44
Matthew 19:23	51
Matthew 20:26–28	26
Matthew 21:22	98
Matthew 23:12	107
Matthew 24:35–36, 44	89
Matthew 25:29	75
Matthew 25:31–46	52
Matthew 26:26–28	27
Matthew 26:39	45
Matthew 27:46	54
Matthew 28:19	28
Mark 6:50b	98
Mark 7:21–23	108
Mark 9:37	90
Mark 9:41	45
Mark 10:51	109
Mark 11:24	113
Mark 12:28–31	2
Mark 14:36	14
Mark 14:61–62	29
Luke 4:13	76
Luke 6:27–28	55
Luke 6:31	65
Luke 6:37	46
Luke 6:41	55
Luke 10:2	30
Luke 12:6–7	76
Luke 12:8	16
Luke 12:15	66
Luke 12:22–24	100
Luke 12:34	100
Luke 12:48	95
Luke 13:30	107
Luke 15:7	56

Luke 15:11–32	67
Luke 16:13	3
Luke 17:17–18	85
Luke 18:24–25	51
Luke 21:1–4	91
Luke 23:34	16–47
Luke 24:13–35	16
John 1:14	31
John 1:38–39	4
John 3:16	1
John 3:36	5
John 5:24	5
John 6:35	32
John 6:44	6
John 6:51	32
John 15:16a	18
John 21:25	40
Acts 2:28	68
Acts 2:32	47
Acts 3:19	57
Acts 7:60	69
Acts 15:22	48
Acts 17:30	57
Romans 2:16	33
Romans 5:19	77
Romans 6:8	18
Romans 6:23	69
Romans 7:19	49
Romans 8:15	19
Romans 8:18	34
Romans 8:26–27	40
Romans 11:33	7
Romans 12:4–5	58
Romans 12:18	114
Romans 13:9–10	8
1 Corinthians 2:9	20
1 Corinthians 3:16	114

1 Corinthians 9:24	101
1 Corinthians 10:13	110
1 Corinthians 12:4–6	92
1 Corinthians 13:1, 13	102
1 Corinthians 15:22–23	86
1 Corinthians 15:55	34
1 Corinthians 16:13	102
2 Corinthians 3:5	21
2 Corinthians 3:17	35
2 Corinthians 9:6–7b	78
2 Corinthians 10:18	21
Galatians 3:28	93
Galatians 5:22–23	79
Galatians 6:9	110
Ephesians 2:8	116
Ephesians 5:25	49
Ephesians 6:13	111
Philippians 2:10–11	9
Philippians 2:14	60
Philippians 3:20	36
Philippians 4:6–7	103
Colossians 2:8	60
Colossians 3:2	36
Colossians 3:13–14	50
Colossians 3:17	87
1 Thessalonians 4:13	71
1 Thessalonians 5:9	10
1 Thessalonians 5:16–18	87
1 Thessalonians 5:22	72
2 Thessalonians 2:3	11
1 Timothy 1:14b	61
1 Timothy 5:17	116
2 Timothy 1:7	104
2 Timothy 3:12	112
2 Timothy 3:16	37
Hebrews 11:3	11
Hebrews 12:7	62

Hebrews 13:2	38
Hebrews 13:6	104
James 1:22	22
James 2:13	72
James 2:14, 16, 26	12
1 Peter 1:24–25	62
1 Peter 5:8	73
2 Peter 3:18	13
1 John 2:3	63
1 John 2:15	94
3 John 1:4	105
Revelation 1:19	88
Revelation 3:16	39

FOREWORD

Our lives are literally filled with language. Sometimes words disappear from our attention immediately like a baseball pitcher's fastball. Other words stick and stay. Think about your reading or your recent conversations. How often do we miss the point as our mind either wanders away or pounces on a small detail? Do we find it necessary to go back and reread that paragraph or wish that our friend would repeat what was just said? When we hear or read the Word of God the same holds true. Sometimes we hear or remember nothing. Other times a single word or phrase may capture our attention. Understanding fully and deeply what we read and hear is a challenge and a great gift. Comprehending the Word of God in a way that we come to know and love God, others and ourselves in a more personal way is a great blessing.

    Greg Hadley presents us with this blessing. He meditates on scripture with the eyes of his mind and also with the eyes of his soul. For Greg the living Word of God is a rich source of inspiration and nourishment. His journey in the Word of God is a very personal journey. This is the gift and blessing he shares with the reader. More than this, we are offered his thoughts, feelings and prayers on the Word of God. Greg provides us with an example of how we can develop a faithful and frequent habit of being with scripture thoughtfully and prayerfully. Reading between lines, you will often see the enthusiasm and inspiration Greg is taking from God's Word. Sacred scripture can be likened to a treasure buried in a field. The treasure remains buried until, through diligent mining, it is discovered and brought forth into the light of day. Greg shares with the reader his attempts to find the essence of God's Word and the mining techniques he employs in the pages of this powerful little book.

The Catechism of the Catholic Church reminds us: "The Christian faith is not a religion of the book. Christianity is the religion of the Word of God—not a written and mute word, but incarnate and living. If scriptures are not to remain a dead letter, Christ, the eternal Word of the living God, must, through the Holy Spirit, open our minds to understand the Scriptures." (Number 180). Greg is obviously mindful of this task. He certainly tries to cooperate with the graces of the Holy Spirit to help the reader journey through the scripture passages selected for this book. The challenge for Greg—and for all of us—is to journey through sacred scripture, digest the Word of God and let God's inspiration guide us through life. A good friend of mine once told me, "The Word of God is a tough nut to crack. Thanks be to God for the Spirit who is a great nutcracker!"

Father Richard Berg, CSC
Portland, Oregon

PREFACE

Readers should first know what this book is—and what it isn't.

During my adult life, I have had many opportunities to learn about the Bible, the "library of God's word." Since my youth, I have believed that it is the inspired word of God, provided to help each of us as we travel along our personal life journeys. As I received instruction, attended Bible studies and spent private time reading the Old and New Testaments, I found inspiring passages that resonated and stuck with me. These words embraced my heart and touched my soul with their insight or lessons I could apply to daily life. Sacred scripture is fresh and alive. I often receive new inspiration from familiar passages. This book is partly about sharing these vibrant passages with readers, and explaining my thoughts, feelings and reactions.

The scriptures I chose would probably be different from those you might select. Even if my selections resonate as much with you and they do with me, they might affect you in an entirely different way. Our backgrounds, life experiences, religious training, associations with others and a general state of mind are all different, and change the particulars of our response to God's word. In grammar school I was taught by the sisters of St. Joseph of Carondolet. My high school years were spent under the watchful eyes of the Christian Brothers of St. John the Baptist De La Salle. The Jesuit Fathers oversaw my four years of university. Active participation in my parish churches in the years since has provided even more opportunities for Bible instruction and study, both as a student and as a teacher. Yet, that does not make me a Bible "scholar" or "expert." Someone with extensive historical education or knowledge of Greek, Aramaic, Hebrew and Latin may meet the minimum requirements for being an expert.

Likewise, my entire life has been spent as an observant Roman Catholic—but I don't consider this to be a "Catholic" book. Any Christian can find spiritual value in these pages.

My understanding of sacred scripture is formed by the Magisterium of the Catholic Church. I believe the Bible was written with the inspiration of the Holy Spirit, and also that it cannot always be accepted literally or historically—but is filled with stories, messages and directions for how each of us may live our earthly life. This book is about my personal, visceral reactions to my favorite passages of scripture. My writing does not have the approval of any Church authority. If I have written anything at odds with the official teaching of the Catholic Church, I take full responsibility. It would never be my intention to stray from church teaching. This book is intended as a highly personal reflection about certain scripture passages and how they have directed and affected my life. You will see that many of the passages I selected are used to assist with an examination of my conscience. May you find value in them, too, and however it may come to you.

You should also know what this book is not intended to be. It is not a Bible commentary. I do not have the competence to tell you what the Bible means. I can only tell you how certain portions of the Bible *have affected me personally* and how scripture has conditioned my outlook on life. Neither is it a credo of beliefs but a compilation of *feelings and stories* as scripture accompanied me on my own spiritual pathway.

A word on my selections. You will find more New Testament scripture than Old Testament scripture. This compendium does not mean that other portions of scripture are not as important to me. Some parts of the Bible are more difficult for me to comprehend or decipher. Nor is this book a completely original and unique text. Over my seventy-plus years, I have heard a substantial number of homilies, attended many retreats and read countless books and Catholic periodicals. I have internalized certain concepts, ideas and other spiritual input during my life. This body of knowledge has become an instinctive part of my thought process. I will provide attribution whenever I quote from someone else's work. If you find passages originated by someone else, I beg forgiveness. Any such oversights were strictly unintentional and if you inform me of the error I will attribute it in any subsequent editions of this book.

I have organized the scripture passages and my responses into four sections.

- God, who is deserving of our praise and adoration;
- God, extending his mercy, compassion, and forgiveness;
- God, entitled to our thanks for his many blessings;
- God, generously accepting our petitions.

My criteria for categorization are solely my feelings about the passage. As a young man I was taught the acronym ACTS to help me with my personal prayer life. Those letters stood for: **A**doration, **C**ontrition, **T**hanksgiving and **S**upplication. If each of my prayers contained elements of adoration for my Creator, contrition for my sins, thanksgiving for the blessing I had received, and supplications for the things that I needed in my life, then my prayer was complete. The four segments of this book reflect a similar concept for using scripture as a vehicle for prayer.

Finally, this is not a book to read front to back. I hope you will browse until you find a passage that is important to you. Please read what I have to say about the scripture. Determine if you have any feelings that match mine. That would make me happy, but it is really not important. Determine your own reaction. Reflect on how this idea can possibly change your outlook or your life for the better. Figure out if your thoughts will help you love God more fully, your neighbor as yourself, or to build the kingdom of God. May the words of sacred scripture convey special blessings on all who read this book.

ACKNOWLEDGEMENTS

My wife, Evie, and I have lived at Mary's Woods at Marylhurst, a retirement community in Lake Oswego, Oregon, since December 2005. Mary's Woods is owned by the Sisters of the Holy Names of Jesus and Mary (SNJM), a Catholic order of nuns. The sisters have created a sanctuary in which seniors live out their final years. Don't get me wrong; this is not a place to curl up and die. Mary's Woods is full of vibrant, bright, active people who thoroughly enjoy life and use their considerable talents and skills to live life to the fullest. We love being here and are continuously impressed with our many accomplished friends and neighbors.

Besides us lay people (less than one-third of the residents are Catholic), Mary's Woods is home to a fairly large group of retired nuns. These sisters are almost universally friendly, loving, kind, and caring. They are also very ecumenical and welcome everyone into the Mary's Woods community with equal enthusiasm. This book has been principally inspired by all the wonderful friends we have made among the sisters. We join them frequently in the chapel for daily Mass. Their simple, honest and open faith is an inspiration to us. As I meet and talk with the sisters, I have been humbled by their sincere commitment to their Lord, His mother, and St. Joseph, His foster father. While they can all be described as "holy women," they do not wear their religion on their sleeves, preferring to give witness by their quiet but cheerful example. *I love the sisters*!

I must also acknowledge, in a special way, the contribution made to this book by Sr. Joan Hansen, SNJM, who contributed its afterword.

Equally inspiring to me is our chaplain, Father Richard Berg, CSC. A Holy Cross father who resides at the University of Portland, Fr. Dick comes to Mary's Woods most days to celebrate

Mass, provide the sacraments, visit the sick and bury the dead. Fr. Dick is uniquely suited for this ministry. He is exceedingly kind and cheerful, has sincere empathy for the elderly, especially the infirm, and is totally self-effacing in his personality. I have the greatest admiration, respect and fondness for this man. As priest, he is devout but not officious; his preaching is thought-provoking but not overblown. His liturgies are uplifting, and they inspire a prayerful response. We are so fortunate to have him as our chaplain.

We have many wonderful friends at Mary's Woods. I attend a men's Bible study twice a month. These men—mostly Protestants—are some of the finest men I have ever met. They are sincerely searching for their God and Savior, are tolerant of everyone and open to new ideas about the ways to achieve their personal salvation. I truly love these men; I count many of them as my best friends.

Of course, my wife is my primary inspiration. She is probably uncomfortable with this adulation but, by her example, much of my own work is possible. Thank you, Evie, for your faithful love over the many years of our marriage (fifty-one and counting) and your wonderful service as mother to our most loved six children.

I must also acknowledge someone else. Sarah Cypher, my editor, is the one who keeps my writing focused, effective and properly constructed. Special prayers of thanks must be given to all editors whose job it is to keep writers like me humble and well connected to our writing deficiencies.

So, in summary, thank you, dear SNJM sisters, Father Dick, Sr. Joan, my Bible study friends, Evie and Sarah. Without you all, this book would not have been possible.

ADORATION

John 3:16

For God so loved the world that he gave his only Son, so that everyone who believes in him might not perish but might have eternal life.

> This is where it all starts... Mankind was wandering around aimlessly until God the Father sent Jesus Christ. This was much more than a gift; it was an awesome act of love to each of us. He did not come in the form of a king, but as a helpless baby. He was not dressed in finery, but in rags. His place of arrival was not some grand palace, but a stable. He was not surrounded by princes, presidents, and world leaders, but by poor workers.
>
> Just think of it! God Almighty takes the form of a man—and a poor one, at that—to open the gates of heaven for all mankind. I could contemplate this mystery forever and still not be able to grasp its nature.

Genesis 1:31a

God looked at everything he had made, and he found it very good.

> I saw a poster in a church hall during the 1980s that said, "God doesn't make junk." Sometimes we see children and adults who have been terribly malformed since birth. Often we are so put off by their disfigurement that we cannot see through it to the human being inside the body. I have encountered such people, and am disquieted by my unease around them. How do I get past the deformity to the *person*?

The same applies to people with mental illness and debilitating illnesses. On one level, I would just like them to go away so I didn't have to deal with my own feelings of discomfort.

This verse leads me to consider another issue. What am I to think of homosexuals? Is their apparently disordered sexual activity something that is a basic part of their DNA? Are these people created by God with this predilection? We don't know the answer to that question yet. But, what if?

I find that I have many basic prejudices and preconceptions, and ask the Lord's help to see things the way they really are, not the way I think they are. May the Lord show me how to get past physical deformity to my neighbor's soul, and give me grace.

Mark 12:28-31

One of the scribes…asked him, "Which is the first of all the commandments?" Jesus replied, "The first is this: 'Hear, O Israel! The Lord our God is Lord alone! You shall love the Lord your God with all your heart, with all your soul, with all your mind, and with all your strength.' The second is this: 'You shall love your neighbor as yourself.' There is no other commandment greater than these."

Are all God's commands to us, "Thou shalt not…?"

Too many of us hold a negative image of being a Christian. If you grew up with a Christian education, you may have felt hemmed in by all the things you could not do or must avoid in life. It is true that the Bible and traditional church teachings spell out many things we are to do, and not do, to be disciples of Jesus. But given the chance to name the most important commandments, Jesus was unequivocal. He tells us to love God with every part of our being, and to love our neighbor as ourselves. There is nothing else nearly as important.

These are simple and straightforward commands. Unfortunately, they are easier said than done. Loving God with my whole being means I must suppress my tendencies to love a lot of other alluring things in this world. I am in a constant turmoil with myself about loving God with great intensity.

The love of one's neighbor is fraught with problems, too. First, some people just don't seem like any neighbor of mine. How am I to love them when they say they hate me and want to destroy my life, family, and country?

Jesus says these two rules for life are all. I must pray with deep humility and sincerity that God will send me the grace necessary to follow them. Without His help, I don't think I have the spiritual strength to do what He asks of me.

Luke 16:13

No servant can serve two masters. He will either hate one and love the other, or be devoted to one and despise the other. You cannot serve God and mammon.

My human nature is in a continual tug-of-war between, on the one hand, loving God with my whole being, and loving life with its blandishments of power, money, fame, and pleasure on the other hand.

Mammon, the evil embodiment of all earthly charms and allurements is constantly in my face. Television, books, newspapers, magazines, billboards, radio—they all shout at me that life would be better if I possessed more earthly wealth, beauty, happiness, and leisure. Yet I am called to love God with my whole mind, my whole heart, and my whole spirit.

You see, it is often easier to cherish and seek the things we can see, touch, taste, feel and hear—the things of this world. To love God can seem more difficult if we cannot see, touch, or hear Him directly. But we each must ask: Which master will I serve?

To serve God wholeheartedly requires cooperation with the graces the Lord provides. It also demands daily discipline, prayer, and total reliance on God to help keep life in perspective. I pray that the Holy Spirit not abandon me in my weaknesses, and that the Lord helps me choose the wiser master.

John 1:38–39

Jesus turned and saw them following him and said to them, "What are you looking for?" They said to him, "Rabbi [which translates to Teacher], where are you staying?" He said to them, "Come, and you will see." So they went and saw where he was staying, and they stayed with him that day. It was about four in the afternoon.

Very early in His public life, Jesus was teaching and attracting many people who were intrigued by what He said. Can you imagine the embarrassment of the two disciples who were following Jesus when He turned and said to them, "What are you looking for?" They stammered out an answer, "Where are you staying?" Jesus said to them, "Come, and you will see."

This is the point: These disciples thought they were deciding to follow this young teacher, Jesus. We do the same thing when we have a spiritual epiphany and decide to follow the Lord. In reality, Jesus says to us, "Come and I will show you where I live and what I am about." In other words, Jesus chooses us; we do not choose Him.

John 3:36 and 5:24

Whoever believes in the Son has eternal life, but whoever disobeys the Son will not see life, but the wrath of God remains upon him.

Amen, amen, I say to you, whoever hears my word and believes in the one who sent me has eternal life and will not come to condemnation.

When one reads sacred scripture, it seems to me, there are two ideas that must be reconciled. First, is there any factual or historical basis to conclude that the Bible was actually written and represents a close approximation of the authors' original words? I say, even the most skeptical observer will find plentiful and credible information indicating that the Bible was written. Non-scholars can locate massive amounts of data that support its authenticity.

Second, the God-given gift of faith must live in the spirit of the reader, since some of what we examine cannot be explained or understood in human terms. These two short passages from John demonstrate my premise. I stipulate that these words were written by St. John (or some close associate) sometime during the first century. As they say, "You can look it up."

But what is the message that tests my faith? Well, Jesus is called the Son of Man—God. One passage tells me that if I merely believe in the Son, I will have eternal life. In other words, through faith, I believe that my soul is immortal. After my earthly death, I will live on forever, I hope in the presence of God Almighty Who is perfect love. Yet the other passage also warns me that love and belief in the Son of Man must be coupled with living out God's commands.

I cannot expect an immortal life of perfect bliss just by loving the Son. I must also observe the things He has instructed me to do—love my neighbor, care for the poor, follow the Golden Rule, and be willing to take up my cross daily and follow Him. Doing these things can only happen if I cooperate with the graces God sends to me daily. While the task may be difficult, the reward is inconceivable.

John 6:44

No one can come to me unless the Father who sent me draw him, and I will raise him on the last day.

Each person must rely on God the Father to help him or her find Jesus Christ. I cannot find Him myself by force of will; only through the graces bestowed on me by the Father can I come to know and follow the Lord.

For those who have been abundantly blessed with these graces already, I offer a sincere prayer that their gift may never be lost. For those who reject God or the many who wander aimlessly in search of spiritual meaning, my prayers are even more heartfelt.

Does this passage tell us that Jews, Muslims, Buddhists, Hindus, and other religions have no chance of eternal salvation? I absolutely reject that it does. God's grace is available to all. Even those profusely blessed may find that their spiritual path to eternity winds along a different road. For me, I rely on God the Father to draw me close to Him and His Son, Jesus. I also count on the Lord's words that He will raise me up on the last day. What more could I possibly ask from my God?

Romans 11:33

Oh, the depth of the riches and wisdom and knowledge of God! How inscrutable are his judgments and how unsearchable his ways.

Many of us spend a lifetime trying to figure God out. We pray, read, and contemplate. Just when we think we are starting to make sense of the Almighty, He shows us again that He is divine and we are human.

God is without beginning or end; we are born and then die. He is all loving, all merciful, all just; we are weak humans who often fail at love, do not show mercy to others, and chase after justice. He has a divine intellect and will; we have clouded minds and a free will that often leads us to trouble.

What's more, we often lash out at God when we see pain and suffering in the world. "How could You let all those Africans starve? Why did You send my loved one that fatal cancer? How can You permit millions of babies to be aborted every year?" Why do we waste breath on these futile challenges to God? As scripture says, "How inscrutable are His judgments and how unsearchable His ways."

I pray for the Lord to help me calmly accept our relationship. He is my God; I am His loving, adoring follower. I have faith that He loves me unconditionally and always wants the best for me. For my part, I bumble along in my weak human ways trying to do my best, but often tripping and falling flat on my face. Although I cannot fully experience the depth of the Lord's riches and wisdom, I ask for His support.

Romans 13:9–10

You shall love your neighbor as yourself. Love does no evil to the neighbor; hence, love is the fulfillment of the law.

This exhortation is seen frequently throughout the scriptures. This particular passage seems slightly different to me from the others of its kind. I am drawn to three separate ideas. Who *really* is my neighbor? What does the word *love* mean? In what way does love become the fulfillment of the law?

Thinking about the Body of Christ (discussed also under Romans 12:4–5, Galatians 3:28, and Philippians 3:20) I must conclude that *every single person on this earth* is my neighbor. In human terms, I don't necessarily like this idea. I have neighbors living nearby with whom I interact almost daily, and some of them, I do not like. I cannot sugar-coat my feelings about them. Then there are the faceless hordes throughout the world who have publicly stated their hatred for my country and all its citizens—including me and my family. These "neighbors" of mine have voiced a passionate goal to kill all whom I hold dear. These are some of the neighbors I am told I must love.

What is *love*? In our culture, the word is used to describe a whole range of human emotions. I love pecan pie; I deeply love my spouse; I love my children and grandchildren; I love my close friends and associates. Each love takes on a substantially different meaning, depending on its context. I believe the call to love our neighbor means wishing that no harm to come to them. We don't have to like them, but at the same time, we can mean it when we wish them good health. We may abhor their ideas, but can also agree that they deserve adequate food, clean water, and shelter. *Love* does not have to mean *like*.

Finally, we are told that the true expression of love is the fulfillment of the law. If I have done my best to love God with every fiber of my being and love my neighbor as myself, then I have done the two principal things that God has commanded me to do.

Psalm 9:2–3

I will praise You, Lord, with all my heart; I will declare all Your wondrous deeds. I will delight and rejoice in You; I will sing hymns to Your name, Most High.

The Psalms are beautiful, poetic prayers; I was challenged to select just a few to include in this book.

Because I love to sing in church and often serve as cantor, leading the congregation, I was especially attracted to this passage. When I use my voice in song, I do so in praise of the Lord and all His wondrous deeds. There is an old saying: "Those who sing pray twice." I pray that the Gentle God allows me to continue using the gift of music for as long as possible.

Philippians 2:10–11

...that at the name of Jesus every knee should bend, of those in heaven and on earth, and every tongue confess that Jesus Christ is Lord, to the glory of God the Father.

As a schoolboy, I was taught by the nuns to bow my head reverently every time I heard or said the holy name of Jesus. We were also instructed to genuflect—touching one knee to the ground—every time we entered a Catholic church. These were visible signs of our love and devotion for our Lord and Savior, Jesus Christ.

At one time, every Catholic parish had a Holy Name Society. This was a group of men and boys who gave public honor to the name of Jesus usually by assembling once a month on Sunday morning at Mass. I'm sorry to say that most of these happy traditions have waned in the past few years. A coarsened society is full of people who routinely use the name of Jesus without respect in casual conversation. Holy Name Societies have all but disappeared. Only a few old timers can be seen bowing their head when Jesus' name is proclaimed in church.

I am not judging here, only bemoaning the loss of respect for the name of Jesus. I try to keep some of these traditions alive in my own heart and in my circle of friends. I pray that both my respect for Jesus' holy name and my actions show to all I believe He truly is Lord, and that by honoring Him I give glory to God the Father.

1 Thessalonians 5:9

For God did not destine us for wrath, but to gain salvation through our Lord Jesus Christ.

If you are looking for the Good News of scripture, you can find it in this verse. We are told that God did not send us into this world to experience turmoil, pain, anguish, sin, and wrath, but to gain salvation through Jesus Christ.

I believe this means the Lord wants me to have a happy and productive life that leads to the everlasting bliss with Him in eternity. However, it is easy to become confused by the Lord's intentions. All of us have witnessed good, pious, God-fearing people who seemed to be crushed with illness, poverty, disintegrating families, and generally lousy human lives. God's plan for each of us is inscrutable.

I must pray for those people but focus on the prize, too. The Lord wants me to gain salvation. It's up to me to cooperate with His grace.

2 Thessalonians 2:3
But the Lord is faithful; he will strengthen you and guard you from the evil one.

Like the stock market, life is a series of ups and downs. Not only life in general, but spiritual life in particular.

Haven't all of us grown weary, discouraged or demoralized in our souls, and questioned our relationship with God? I know I have. Sometimes I think I have been making a serious effort, but suddenly discover that God seems missing in my life; perhaps things are going along well when I have an abrupt spiritual meltdown. Why do these things happen?

I believe these meltdowns happen to me when I have lost my vision of God's faithfulness to me. I read this passage and remind myself: He is forever reaching out to me and blessing me endlessly with His grace. His infinite love provides a shield for me from the evil one who roams the world looking for targets to lure into sin.

I pray to gentle Jesus to wrap His arms around me and shelter me. While I sometimes lose touch with Him, I hope that He never loses touch with me.

Hebrews 11:3
By faith we understand that the universe was ordered by the word of God, so that what is visible came into being through the invisible.

I have little trouble believing in God while viewing a sunset in the Rocky Mountains, looking at the Grand Canyon, or observing a star-filled sky on a dark night. And what could be more miraculous than the gestation and birth of a baby? How can you see the exotic fish in the ocean and not believe in God? As St. Thomas Aquinas said, there are seven rational proofs for the existence of a Supreme Being that do not require faith, just observation.

And yet, many people remain unconvinced. Many are more than willing to credit a Big Bang for starting the universe, without also stipulating that the original matter for the Big Bang came from our Creator. I truly believe the Lord's invisible presence is not limited by time. Nothing existed before Him, and nothing shall come after Him. The visible things of this world came forth from His invisible hand.

I thank the Father God for the beautiful world He has given to us for our use. Let's pray that He also remind us to respect the planet, be conscious of our effect on the environment, and use all worldly resources in a respectful and conscientious way.

James 2:14, 16, 26

What good is it, my brothers, if someone says he has faith but does not have works? Can that faith save him? So faith of itself, if it does not have works, is dead. For just as a body without a spirit is dead, so also faith without works is dead.

Please be gentle with me, my Christian friends, who firmly believe in the concept of *solo fide*. I know you believe that "faith only" is necessary for salvation and I respect your position, which dates to the Protestant Reformation.

Is it correct to believe that God the Son, Jesus the Christ, took on human form, conducted a public ministry, eventually suffered, died, was buried, and resurrected from the dead? Yes! Does His action, in and of itself, open the gates of heaven to all believers? Yes! Is it enough to proclaim that when one accepts Jesus Christ as a personal Lord and Savior, this is sufficient for receiving saving salvation? St. James says no.

As an individual I can proclaim my unshakeable belief in Jesus Christ—and I do. But I think I am called to live out that belief by my actions here on earth. Matthew 25 is clear about the need to help the lowly, visit the imprisoned, welcome strangers, and care for all God's human creatures no matter how humble or insignificant they may be. Faith in Jesus Christ is absolutely necessary—but it is not adequate, in my belief. We must actively participate in the building of the kingdom here on earth and that is accomplished by our humble, human works showing love for our neighbors.

I am not a theologian and do not wish to debate the grand premise of *solo fide*. I wish I was learned enough to persuade others to accept the need for works. I do not have those skills, but I welcome loving and open-minded discussions with anyone who is similarly inclined.

I especially thank the Lord for my many non-Catholic friends who have been so open, loving, and encouraging to me, and ask Him to bless each of them with abundant grace.

2 Peter 3:18

But grow in grace and in the knowledge of our Lord and savior Jesus Christ. To him be glory now and to the day of eternity. Amen.

I learned at a weekend church retreat that the perfect metaphor for a successful Christian life is a three-legged milking stool.

The three legs are named *piety, study*, and *action*. If any of the three legs break or are missing, the stool becomes unstable, landing us on our rumps. Similarly, our spiritual life must rely on equal amounts of piety, study, and action if we are to maintain a vibrant God-centered existence.

I grow in grace by my pious prayer, a humble reliance on the Lord, and my loving actions toward my neighbor. I grow in knowledge by steadily increasing my understanding of God's word and the teachings of my church. If I am faithful to these three things, I give glory to my Lord not only today but on the day I step across life's threshold into eternal life in the arms of a loving God.

Genesis 3:19b

For you are dirt, and to dirt you shall return.

This verse is the basis for the Ash Wednesday liturgy, when many Christians receive ashes on their foreheads as Lent begins. "Remember, you are dust and to dust you shall return."

Even the old need to be reminded: No one gets out of here alive. Each year we enter the Lenten season promising ourselves that this year, we will get serious about repentance and prepare our souls for the inevitable earthly death that we all must face.

Each person reaches a different level of success with their Lenten commitment, yet it is clear that the declarative statement in Genesis offers no wiggle-room to any of us.

I ask the Lord to help me keep this brief verse ever in my mind. Not as a statement of dread but as a statement of hope. I have been sent to this earth for a purpose. I ask for His assistance in fulfilling the tasks He has assigned to me during my limited time on earth.

Mark 14:36

He said, "Abba, Father, all things are possible to you. Take this cup away from me, but not what I will but what you will."

Elsewhere I comment how I am touched by Jesus' human nature, told in Matthew, when He sees how horrible Good Friday is going to be for Him. While this verse is similar, there is one very important difference that sets its apart from Mark's gospel. Here, Jesus refers to His Father as "Abba." In Aramaic, "Daddy."

How many of us have a mental picture of God the Father as an old man with a flowing white beard and a rather stern countenance? But here, we see Jesus asking His Daddy for relief from what is to come. For me, that one phrase, "Abba," totally changes how I perceive the relationship between God the Father and God the Son. My own adult children call me Dad or Pops or Daddy—and I know it is said with love and endearment. I sense the same feeling between Father God and God the Son.

It gives me courage to pray to Abba, knowing that my heavenly Dad loves me intently and will listen to my requests. During times in my life when God seems remote from me, I always direct my prayer to Abba knowing that He will smile and put His arm around me as I tell Him what I need in my life.

Numbers 6:24–26

The Lord bless and keep you! The Lord let His face shine upon you, and be gracious to you! The Lord look upon you kindly and give you peace.

I love this passage. Priests and celebrants often use these words at the end of Mass as a final blessing before dismissal. Look at all the wonderful things the blessing calls down from heaven for me: the Lord's blessings; that God will keep me close to Him; that I might see God's face shine upon me; that God be gracious to me, look upon me kindly and give me peace.

What a comprehensive and beautiful blessing this is. I feel so loved and so fortunate when I hear these words, and I bow my head in loving adoration, praise, and thanksgiving.

Luke 12:8

I tell you, everyone who acknowledges me before others the Son of Man will acknowledge before the angels of God.

Have you ever been questioned by a friend, "Do you accept Jesus Christ as your personal Lord and Savior?" Do you stammer a tongue-tied response as your cheeks flush in sudden embarrassment? Why are we so taken off guard by such statements, especially from our friends who attend evangelical churches?

There is just something about wearing our religion on our sleeve that makes us squirm with discomfort. Our confident response, of course, should be, "Yes, I accepted Jesus Christ as my Savior when I was baptized and I have tried to live out that commitment to Him ever since. How about you?"

But it is not just in these bold statements that we acknowledge our Lord before others. Our actions speak louder than words. A cheerful, compassionate person who obviously cares for his or her neighbor shows, by example, what it means to be a true follower of Christ. I once heard during a retreat the rhetorical question, "If they put you on trial for being a follower of Christ, would there be enough evidence to convict you?" I can acknowledge Jesus by both my words and actions. By doing so, I am confident that Jesus will keep His word and will acknowledge me before the angels of God.

Luke 24:13–35

The appearance of Jesus on the road to Emmaus.
(For complete scripture text, see endnotes).

These final verses of St. Luke's Gospel are one of my favorite parts of the scripture. I like it because, in these few verses, I see the basic conversion story most of us must experience during our life.

We see two of Christ's followers returning home from Jerusalem to Emmaus, about eight miles away. In the past few days, their dreams have been shattered; Jesus, the supposed messiah for whom they had awaited, has been tried and crucified. They are disconsolate as they walk along the road discussing the disappointing and devastating turn of events. Suddenly they encounter a man traveling along the same road, a stranger. The stranger asks what they are talking about.

The two men cannot believe that everyone has not heard of the momentous events in Jerusalem during the past few days—but with great authority, the stranger begins to show the two men how the events have been foretold in scripture and that the man, Jesus, is indeed the Messiah, the Son of God. They listen in rapt attention as the stranger explains everything. When they have reached their destination, the stranger plans to continue on but the two men beg him to stay and tell them more. They take a meal together and when the stranger takes bread, blesses it, and gives it to them, the two men immediately recognize him as Jesus, the Lord. The two men rush back to Jerusalem bearing the good news.

A thrilling story! I began following Jesus as a youngster but didn't really understand why. Then a variety of teachers gave me eyes to see, ears to hear, and a heart to understand the story of Jesus' redeeming incarnation, His passion, death, and resurrection that opened the gates of heaven for me. For me! And when did I most clearly recognize Jesus? In the breaking of the bread, the Eucharist.

I ask the Lord today to let me continuously live out the experience of the two men on the road to Emmaus and let me always recognize His sacred presence whenever I am privileged to receive the Holy Eucharist.

John 15:16a

It was not you who chose Me, but I who chose you…

This is one of my favorites. Most of us, if we experience some type of spiritual conversion, think it is because of something we did or that we were especially cooperative with God's graces.

I experienced a big epiphany in 1969. I considered the event as life-changing. Looking back, I rationalized that I had been ready to change and, given the opportunity, I could influence others for Christ by using my talents to build up the Lord's kingdom on earth. In other words, I believed I had chosen God at that moment in my life.

Jesus showed me that I had it backwards. He let me find this passage in John's gospel so I could see how things really worked. Though I may often fail in the role of Jesus' follower, I will not again forget who blessed me with grace to be His disciple. It was He.

Romans 6:8

If, then, we have died with Christ, we believe that we shall also live with him.

In many churches, including newer Catholic churches, provision has been made for immersion baptism. The symbolism for the new Christian is clear. To become a follower of Jesus Christ you must descend into the tomb with Him and then be resurrected with him also. The form calls for the person to go down into the depths of the baptismal font followed by rising from the water and climbing the steps on the other side of the font. Death followed by resurrection. Resurrection followed by eternal life in the Presence of God.

This powerful symbol conveys the essence of being a Christian. Life may not always be easy and eventually all us must die. But that is not the end; just the beginning. A pious life, lived loving God and loving neighbor, is rewarded with eternal happiness because of the graces provided by Christ's obedient sacrifices for each of us.

I do believe that I shall one day live with the Lord. I pray that He continues to shower me with His graces, and gives me the strength to live in the glorious sunshine of His love.

Romans 8:15

For you did not receive a spirit of slavery to fall back into fear, but you received a spirit of adoption, through which we cry, 'Abba, Father.'

I am told that if I am led by the Spirit, I will be a child of God. The Lord says, "I don't want you to be full of fear or think of yourself as a slave." What God really wants for me is to feel He has adopted me. As a child, He wants me to call Him "Daddy."

And, as an adopted child of God, I am also an heir. All I must do to receive my inheritance is to willingly accept whatever earthly sufferings are sent my way. Then I will be glorified with Jesus in eternal life.

I feel so fortunate that the Lord has added me to His family as an adopted child. When I reflect on this passage I will always think of myself with His arms around me as I look adoringly into His eyes, proclaiming, "I love you, Daddy."

1 Corinthians 2:9

But as it is written: "What eye has not seen, and ear has not heard, and what has not entered the human heart, what God has prepared for those who love him."

While visiting dying friends and relatives, I have often used this scripture. Sitting at a deathbed, I have observed the physical pain and anguish of a person's final days or hours of their lives.

The verse may sound preachy to someone experiencing intense agony during the last stage of cancer. But, I believe God will take us to a better place after we breathe our last breath. A place so wonderful, in fact, that we cannot contemplate the grandeur with our frail human capability.

This idea is like a torch that I should always hold in front of me as I travel through life towards human death.

Psalm 23:1–6

The Lord is my shepherd; there is nothing I lack. In green pastures You let me graze; to safe waters You lead me; You restore my strength. You guide me along the right path for the sake of Your name. Even when I walk through a dark valley, I fear no harm for You are at my side; Your rod and staff give me courage. You set a table before me as my enemies watch; You anoint my head with oil, my cup overflows. Only goodness and love will pursue me all the days of my life; I will dwell in the house of the Lord for years to come.

Certain scripture needs little comment. Psalm 23 is one of those. How often we hear these words, especially at funerals and memorial services. But the verses apply to all times of our lives.

I ask the Lord to help me experience hope and comfort every time I hear or read Psalm 23. May I feel His steady hand and loving embrace in each word of this scripture. He is so generous.

2 Corinthians 3:5

Not that of ourselves we are qualified to take credit for anything, as coming from us; rather, our qualification comes from God.

It is very easy to be filled with pride as I exercise my gifts. I may be a fine author, wonderful singer, talented painter, terrific woodworker or mechanic, great athlete, and sought-after public speaker. What I often forget is that my gifts, whatever they are, and however abundant they are, do not belong to me.

They have been given, or loaned, to me by God. He expects me to use these gifts to build up his kingdom and help in the salvation journey we all may travel. So, when I am inclined to pat myself on the back for my talents, I must remember who really deserves all the credit.

I ask the Lord to instill in me a sense of humility.

2 Corinthians 10:18

For it is not the one who recommends himself who is approved, but the one whom the Lord recommends.

A recent prayer: "Lord, take a look at me. Lately, I've been going to church real regularly. I have also been helping out a lot around the parish, pitching in where needed. Did I tell you, Lord, that I have also been visiting the sick once in awhile? Oh, by the way, we have been putting an extra five dollars in the collection basket each Sunday, too. Well, I guess You already knew that stuff about me already, Lord, but just in case, I wanted to give you an update on how I'm doing."

I think I just wasted a few moments of God's time. Yup, He already knew all that stuff. And it is pretty clear that my self-promotion doesn't do much to advance my cause. If the Lord knows the number of hairs on my head, then I'm quite sure He knows everything else about me, too.

A better prayer: "Lord, help me to remember the things I need to do in order to seek Your recommendation. Love of God, love of neighbor, keeping Your commandments and statutes all represent a pretty good start. I need to be reminded constantly, Lord, how much You already love and look over me each day."

James 1:22

Be doers of the word and not hearers only, deluding yourselves…

We can deceive ourselves into thinking that we completely hear "the word" on Sunday mornings at church. But this brief verse is unequivocal about what I am called to do and to be, every day.

Some of what I hear in the Bible does not appeal to my feeble human nature. I am willing to hear it; I just don't want to act on it. But I know that is not God's plan for me. His word tells us to act upon it. When we hear that we must love God with our entire being, we must listen and obey. When told that we need to love our neighbors as ourselves, we cannot be selective about which neighbors to love.

I must be a doer—not just a pew-sitting, dues-paying sermon-listener. I pray to the Father to give me the grace to live out my Christian discipleship on a minute-to-minute basis, accomplishing those things to build His kingdom and be His faithful follower.

Ecclesiastes 3:1–8

There is an appointed time for everything, and a time for every affair under the heavens. A time to be born, and a time to die; a time to plant, and a time to uproot the plant. A time to kill, and a time to heal; a time to tear down, and a time to build. A time to weep, and a time to laugh; a time to mourn, and a time to dance. A time to scatter stones, and a time to gather them; a time to embrace, and a time to be far from embraces. A time to seek, and a time to lose; a time to keep, and a time to cast away. A time to rend, and a time to sew; a time to be silent; and a time to speak. A time to love, and a time to hate; a time of war, and a time of peace.

Of all the Old Testament passages, I believe this one evokes the most contemplative reflection. Each time one reads or hears these words, fresh new meanings unfold.

Depending on current events, I can find encouragement here. What time is it in my life? Nearing the time to die? Is it the time to end war and find peace? Or perhaps it is time to laugh and be happy? I have been silent; is it now time to speak up? When I think about my life, my response to the juxtaposed statements can vary widely depending on timing and personal circumstances.

I pray that the Father keeps me on an even keel. Through His grace, I seek to be even-handed and temperate in all my reactions to the world around me. I ask that He bless me with calmness, a sense of steady purpose, and complete trust in His plan for my life.

Matthew 5:16

Your light must shine before others, that they may see your good deeds and glorify your heavenly Father.

This passage leads me to ponder the emergency responders during the World Trade Center attacks of

2001. Many brave men and women entered that black, smoky cauldron to help others find safety. Using flashlights in the ominously dark stairwells, the fire and police officers led people away from death in the inferno.

This seems an apt metaphor for shining a spiritual light into others' lives, and guiding them from sin, into the arms of a loving God. When I am given the opportunity to assist others, I must become the flashlight that illuminates their way—but first I must recognize the opportunity to do so.

I pray for the Lord's help in being a beacon for others who need help along the road to Christ. Just as important, I need help sensing when He is calling me to shine a light for others.

Matthew 13:1–9

The Parable of the Sower.
(For complete scripture text, see endnotes).

> The farmer is sowing seeds. Some fall on the pathway, where they are scooped up by the birds. Some fall on rocky ground, where there is little soil, and when the sun rises, the virtually rootless seeds wither and die. Some seeds fall among the thorns, where they grow, but are eventually choked by the thorns. But some seeds fall on good ground where they produced one hundred or sixty or thirty-fold.
>
> Having made his point, Jesus said to the assembled crowd, "Those who have ears should listen." We know the seed is the word of God. While it is broadcast to many, only some are positively affected. A few listen but quickly fall away. Others are initially influenced but then have their faith choked out by the cares of life. When God's word reaches receptive hearts, there can be a great building up of the kingdom.

I must be careful when hearing this parable, for it can make me feel judgmental. I have been blessed that God's word has touched me and has borne fruit. I must constantly remind myself that the gift of faith I have been given was neither earned by me nor deserved. The seed thrown on me does not somehow make me better than the pathway, the rocky soil, or the thorns.

It is too easy to say, "See how I have born fruit? Those other poor wretches had their chance but did not take advantage." This is a terrible mistake! God gifted me from the beginning. Now, I must seek out those who lived on the pathways, on rocky ground, or among the thorns and see if I can share some of my bounty with them. This is what Jesus is calling me to do, and I must not fail to heed His call to help my neighbors.

Matthew 18:20

For where two or three are gathered together in my name, there I am in the midst of them.

This is a profound passage. Whenever I am in the role of a prayer leader in a small group of people, I quote these words. Whether the venue is a hospital room, a family home, a sandy beach, or a care center for the elderly, Jesus becomes present to those who pray together invoking His name.

As family members gather around a dying, elderly patient in a seedy rest home to bid a final farewell, the room may not look like a cathedral. Yet, Jesus is in the midst of them; He said so Himself. He provides us with consolation, strength, necessary graces, a sense of peace, and whatever else we need. We hold hands and have a strong sense of His presence in our little circle. At this moment, He is not a mysterious, unknown God. He is right there.

I give thanks to the Lord Jesus for being present to us when we call him.

Matthew 20:26–28

Whoever wishes to be great among you shall be your servant; whoever wishes to be first among you shall be your slave. Just so, the Son of Man did not come to be served but to serve and to give his life as a ransom for many.

We have all seen sports fans on TV chanting, "We're number one!" after their team has won an important game. In daily life, I suppose all of us like to be number one most of the time. We like to be the first served in a restaurant. It's great to be placed at the head table for a banquet. We feel superior when selected for a promotion at work.

I have experienced these human feelings, too. Let me be the boss. I will be in charge. You are expected to follow my directions. Do my bidding and serve at my pleasure. Then we hear Jesus say: "No, you have that backwards. It is your job to serve others, to put yourself in the position of a slave."

Jesus was not incarnated as a mighty potentate or prince. He led a humble life, sought out the poor and disenfranchised, and associated with sinners and tax collectors. When the time came "to give His life as a ransom for many," he did not hesitate. He continued to serve others right up to His death on the cross.

Am I not called to do the same thing during my life? I believe Jesus calls me to service—service to God the Father, my family, my friends, and my neighbors. I am called to be number two, not number one. I need the Lord to remind me of this call on a frequent basis, for it is too easy for me to forget what position I am to seek in this life.

Matthew 26:26–28

While they were eating, Jesus took bread, said the blessing, broke it, and giving it to them, saying, "Take and eat; this is my body." Then he took a cup, gave thanks, and gave it to them, saying, "Drink from it, all of you, for this is my blood of the covenant, which will be shed on behalf of many for the forgiveness of sins."

These words spoken by Jesus on the night before his passion and death provide the basis for the great prayer of the Roman Catholic Church, the Mass.

These words of consecration change simple bread and wine into the body and blood of Jesus Christ. Each day thousands of ordained priests celebrate Mass around the world saying similar words to those recorded in this passage.

Why do I believe that bread and wine become the body and blood of Jesus? Because Jesus said so. He further went on to say to his apostles, "Do this is remembrance of Me." Just think; when I attend Mass and receive Holy Communion, I am taking into my hands the body and blood, soul, and divinity of my Lord and Savior Jesus Christ. This fact is almost too awesome for me to contemplate. Even though I intellectually believe this article of my faith, I often lose focus and fail to grasp the significance of what I am doing, and what I am receiving.

I pray to the Lord to give me the graces to worship Him in awe and reverence, remembering always the unbelievable gift He has given me in the Eucharist. I love and praise Him, the mighty Savior.

Matthew 28:19

Go, therefore, and make disciples of all nations, baptizing them in the name of the Father, and of the Son and of the Holy Spirit.

This scripture represents the last words Jesus spoke to His disciples before He ascended into heaven. His command to the eleven apostles is the same one He gives to each of His followers—you and me. He has given us thorough directions and sent the Holy Spirit to grace our work. Now it is up to us to make disciples of all nations.

And yet, some of us seem reluctant to speak openly about our spiritual life and religious beliefs. Remember the old social bromide: "Never discuss politics or religion." I wonder why I am often shy about discussing my faith with friends, let alone a stranger? Am I afraid I will sound self-righteous or high and mighty? Am I afraid I won't be able to adequately answer some question presented to me? Perhaps it is my human fear of rejection.

Like so many of the Bible's verses, God is not making a suggestion to us; it is a command. "Go! Do it! Now!" If I wish to be counted as a follower of Jesus, I have no choice in this. I am not required to travel the world converting souls, but there is a small chunk of the planet on which I can do my work: the one on which I am standing right now.

I need the Lord's grace to overcome this reluctance to share my faith. I ask Him to remind me that He is always there beside me, giving me the right words to say so that I can be His true disciple and continue His work on earth.

Genesis 9:13

I set my bow in the clouds to serve as a sign of the covenant between me and the earth.

I love this part of Genesis for one reason. So many people taunt God and demand a sign from Him. And he answers: "OK, you want a sign? Here, I will give you rainbows. They are My sign that I will never again destroy the earth with flood. I will remind you of My promise many days in the spring and fall of each year, especially when you look to the east."

I thank the Lord for this most brilliant and spectacular sign. Every time I see a rainbow, I am reminded of the many promises He has made to His people. I am most blessed to have a God who speaks to His people with such grandeur.

Mark 14:61–62

And again the high priest asked him and said to him, "Are you the Messiah, the son of the Blessed one?" Then Jesus answered, "I am; and you will see the Son of Man seated at the right hand of the Power and coming with the clouds of heaven."

There is a scene from an old Jack Nicholson film where he is in the witness chair being interrogated by a prosecutor. The attorney makes a vigorous demand of Nicholson: "I want the truth!" With equal vigor, Nicholson replies, "You can't handle the truth!"

Wow! What drama! This scripture passage provides that same kind of tension. It is said in legal situations the prosecutor should never ask a question for which he doesn't already have the answer. In this story, the High Priest thought he knew what response Jesus would give, but he was mistaken. When Jesus said that He was the

Messiah and the Son of Man (God), the High Priest was dumbstruck and furious. The exchange led Jesus to the cross on Calvary.

But, the most important thing for me is the clear and unequivocal way Jesus identifies Himself. In other places in the Bible, Jesus is somewhat more obscure, referring back to writings in the Torah and of the prophets. Here, He clearly states that He is the Messiah the Jews had been waiting for: and He says you will be able to tell because you will see Him seated next to the Father when He comes to judge the earth. That's good enough for me.

As the old saying goes, "Jesus said it and I believe it." One question remains: why is it taking so long for all of us to figure out who Jesus really is?

I ask the Lord for his continued blessing of the gift of faith so that I may always believe He is my Lord and Savior.

Luke 10:2

The harvest is abundant but the laborers are few; so ask the master of the harvest to send out laborers for his harvest.

I often forget to pray that God will send more vocations to the religious life. We urgently need priests, nuns, brothers, ministers, and deacons to shepherd the flocks of believers and also to reach out to non-believers with a message of conversion.

Praying for vocations does not let the lay people off the hook. In the absence of clerics, we must minister to our own religionists (as we are able) and evangelize non-believers. In recent times, lay people felt that the job of finding and converting those in spiritual need was strictly for the priests, nuns, and ministers. But because of dwindling numbers of ordained priests and even ministers, lay people *must* take up their work of feeding those who are hungry for the word of God.

Catholics can volunteer their time and talent to help with the Rite of Christian Initiation of Adults in their parishes. God calls me to this work, even though I often feel I would like to avoid it. I ask for His grace to give me the spirit of evangelization and zeal to spread His word. I accept my obligation to get involved in outreach programs in my own congregation.

John 1:14

And the Word became flesh and made his dwelling among us, and we saw his glory, the glory as of the Father's only Son, full of grace and truth.

Jesus, the Second Person of the Blessed Trinity, is referred to in scripture by many names. In the prologue to John's Gospel, he uses the term, *The Word*, extensively to describe God the Son, in existence from all eternity.

John tells us in this poetic verse that The Word became flesh and dwelt among us as a human being. Both fully divine and fully human, Jesus reflected the Father's glory and was full of grace and truth.

With our weak intellects, full comprehension of this act is impossible. We struggle to accept that Almighty God took the form of a man and came into this world to open the gates of heaven for all of us. Can you believe this? Is it possible to discern how much love God must have for each one of us? The Father sends His Son as gift to every lowly human being, including me. Not only did He come "like us in all things but sin," but He arrived as a helpless baby, birthed in a stable with just poor shepherds to greet Him.

We often exchange gifts at Christmas time to remind us of the gift God the Father sent to us. How insignificant those exchanges of presents really are! I have been given the gift of eternal life by God's only begotten Son. What words of thanks could ever represent an adequate response?

John 6:35, 51

I am the bread of life; whoever comes to me will never hunger, and whoever believes in me will never thirst.

I am the living bread that came down from heaven; whoever eats this bread will live forever; and the bread that I will give is my flesh for the life of the world.

Our human lives can be sustained only if we nourish our bodies regularly and quench our thirst. In these two passages, John quotes Jesus as saying, "I am the bread of life." Expanding on this idea, Jesus tells us that the bread He is talking about is His own flesh given for the life of the world.

During His ministry on earth, Jesus explained this concept to those He taught. Many were turned off by His words. They said, "How can He give us His own flesh to eat? This is a repugnant idea to us!" A lot of followers left Jesus over this issue.

At the Last Supper on Holy Thursday evening, Jesus instituted the Eucharist. Taking bread, He blessed it, broke it and gave to his disciples with the words, "Take and eat; this is My body." At the conclusion of dinner, Jesus blessed the cup of wine and said, "This is the cup of My blood to be shed for the salvation of all people. *Do this in memory of Me."*

The Lord knew that I would need to be sustained in my daily life long after He had departed this earthly world. So Jesus left me this sacred food and drink as a gesture of His deep love for me and all mankind. Each day at Mass when the ordained priest reenacts the events of the Last Supper (saying, "Do this in memory of Me," etc.), the simple bread and wine on the altar are changed to the body, blood, soul and divinity of Jesus Christ. I believe this through the gift of faith my God has given me, and do not have words to explain how awesome it is to me.

I accept Jesus' body and blood as an everlasting commitment of His love and caring for me. I prostrate myself before the Lord God Almighty in worship, adoration, praise, and thanksgiving.

Romans 2:16

For I am not ashamed of the gospel. It is the power of God for the salvation of everyone who believes: for Jew first and then Greek.

The first apostles were not ashamed to preach the Gospel, the good news of Jesus the Christ. Scared, yes, but not ashamed. They came to learn how powerful it was to tell the world about God-made-man, His life, death, resurrection, and ascension to the Father.

The first audience was the Jewish people, followed by Gentiles. Look what this handful of humble apostles was able to accomplish. From these tiny, vulnerable roots of Christianity, many in the world have heard the salvation story of Jesus, including you and me.

How about us? Are we ashamed of the Gospel? Are you and I willing to take up the work begun by the original apostles and continue to spread the good news throughout the world? It is part of God's call to us. If you and I don't do this work, who will?

Let us pray to the Lord for help getting out of our comfort zones to preach the salvation of Jesus Christ. Soap boxes and exhortation are not required. As St. Francis of Assisi told his followers, "Preach the Gospel to all people; if absolutely necessary, you should use words." May the Lord remind us that our example may deliver a more powerful message than any words we could speak. Through His grace we can be faithful apostles.

Romans 8:18

I consider that the sufferings of this present time are as nothing compared with the glory to be revealed for us.

Have you ever visited a cancer patient's ward, Alzheimer's unit, or a critical care section in an emergency hospital? You find yourself surrounded by people experiencing agonizing physical, emotional, psychological, and spiritual suffering. If someone you know or love is admitted there, you intensely share their anguish. At moments like this it seems impossible to see a bright side.

Jesus, in His human nature, must have thought the three hours hanging from the cross on Calvary would never end. He even cried out, "My God, why have you forsaken Me?" At times like this, how can I possibly get my arms around the concept that "the best is yet to come?"

But, so it is! When I am in the depths of my despair, when the pain is at its worst, can I visualize an eternal life—forever and ever—lived in the Glorious presence of my God? That eternal life of bliss is right around the corner for us all. My human nature, while experiencing cruel suffering, might deny the indescribable ecstasy that awaits me on the other side. So I must plead with the Lord to send me the graces to accept God's unbelievable generosity in the next world for those who love Him and follow His commands.

1 Corinthians 15:55

Where, O death, is your victory? Where, O death is your sting?

As I advance into old age, it is inevitable that I must suffer the loss of dearest loved ones, close friends, and esteemed acquaintances. Now, in my mid-seventies, it seems that death has become an old friend, revisiting my world often.

I do my best to keep each death in perspective. "They have gone to a better place," I think. "My dear one is now free of all earthly suffering and is wrapped in God's loving arms." Some losses have caused me grievous pain—my darling sister, Ruth, for example. When I turn to God for personal consolation after such an event, I am graced with the ability to think clearly about what has just happened. The one I love has been taken from this earthly life but now experiences an eternity of heavenly bliss, face-to-face with God.

Because of Jesus, we can all triumph over death, denying it victory over us. Death's sting can be washed away by our human tears of loss.

2 Corinthians 3:17

Now the Lord is the Spirit, and where the Spirit of the Lord is, there is freedom.

My faith is deeply rooted in the belief of a Triune God—Father, Son, and Spirit, three distinct persons in one God. While this is a mystery, it is a bedrock article of my religious credo. So, I have no difficulty accepting this verse.

I am told here that where the Spirit of the Lord is, there, too, is freedom. What does this freedom mean? Some may feel that the commandments and ordinances of God restrict our human freedom. They complain, "I cannot do this and be a loyal follower; I must do these other things to be called a disciple." In truth, there can be no loving relationship between God and humankind without freedom. The Spirit of the Lord blesses me with the gift of free will, allowing me to choose my own path. Will this freedom cause me to make mistakes along the way? Of course! But I have not been predestined to a specific course of action.

Where is there love in God's relationship with me, if I am denied free will? Love and freedom are linked, especially in the relationship between my God and me. I thank His for sending His Spirit into this world and giving me the wonderful gift of freedom.

Philippians 3:20

But our citizenship is in heaven, and from it we also await a savior, the Lord Jesus Christ.

The Body of Christ is made up of people holding citizenship in many different earthly nations. We are diverse and come from every corner of the planet. But that is our secular life: In reality, every one of us has citizenship in heaven.

Our relationship with God transcends where we live on this earth or what country has issued us a passport. We all need to focus on our celestial spiritual home, not our earthly one.

As a citizen of this almighty kingdom, I anticipate the second coming of our Lord and Savior, Jesus Christ. His return to make final judgment on us all causes both fear and awe. Fear because we do not wish to be found wanting. Awe since we know the Lord is coming again, but we know not when.

I pray the Lord blesses me with the ability to put my spiritual citizenship first in my life, and reminds me daily to focus on what's next, not what is happening now.

Colossians 3:2

Think of what is above, not of what is on earth.

This is an elemental spiritual concept. I am told to think of what is above—the afterlife, heaven, an eternity in the presence of God—and not what is on earth. But I *am* on earth and I see a lot of things that are attractive to me.

Riches, pleasure, idle leisure, and a generally easy life all whisper their seductive song into my ears. Yes, I am told, hedonism will surely make you happy. Strive for wealth so that your life can be spent on beaches in Hawaii, restaurants in Manhattan, pleasure palaces in Las Vegas, and cruises to the Bahamas. Then, when you get old, you can return your focus to eternity. You will have wonderful memories in your advancing age.

Oh, what a terrible and false promise! The evil one hopes I will listen and agree. But the Lord has told me that earthly death will come like a thief in the night, showing up when I least expect it. Therefore, I must continually stay focused on eternity, not what is here on earth.

Once again, I pray for the Lord's graces so that I can overcome my human proclivity for things of the world.

2 Timothy 3:16

All scripture is inspired by God and is useful for teaching, for refutation, for correction, and for training in righteousness.

This book has been written by picking and choosing scripture. I confess that not every word in the Bible has inspired me, nor do I totally comprehend how some passages could help me, or others, on our personal salvation journey. But, I do accept that all scripture is inspired by God. Therefore, it must be useful for the purposes stated in this verse from St. Paul's second letter to his friend, Timothy.

To achieve these beneficial outcomes, each person may find different passages to be in some way helpful. Certain parts of the biblical "library" are useful to teach about God. Others will assist in refuting incorrect notions. Still others may inspire greater righteousness. I accept all that, and most important, I state again my absolute belief that all scripture is the inspired word of God.

Let us thank the Holy Spirit for touching the hearts and opening the minds of those who wrote the scriptures. Although the books of the Bible are composed in different literary forms by many different human beings using diverse languages and idiom over thousands of years, the Spirit influenced each and every writer.

I am blessed to be able to read this sacred writing that assists me on my own pathway to salvation. Let these words give me eyes to see, ears to hear and a heart to understand God's message to me.

Hebrews 13:2

Do not neglect hospitality, for through it some have unknowingly entertained angels.

One of my favorite authors is the French Dominican priest, Michel Quoist. His book, *Prayers*, sold over 2.5 million copies. In that book, Fr. Quoist speaks with great eloquence about the concept of hospitality.

I will not quote him directly; the passage I am referring to is much too long for this book. He tells a fictional but compelling story about a rain-filled, windy night when he is alone at home. He opens his front door slightly in response to a knock. Outside he sees several well-dressed strangers seeking relief from the inclement weather. As a matter of hospitality he invited them into his home. There was a second knock. This time many more wanted entrance and this group was comprised of dirty, hungry, and very needy people. The more he let in, the more that pounded on his door demanding entrance.

Finally, Fr. Quoist writes, he was overwhelmed, there was no more room, and he was pleading to God for relief. "Don't worry," said Jesus, "while you were dealing with all these unwanted visitors, I, the Lord, slipped in among them."

I love this story. For a professed Christian, hospitality should be one of my prime virtues. All should be welcomed, and be made to feel comfortable and at ease. How can I hope to evangelize someone if I ignore them or act aloof when they approach? When visiting homeless centers or rest homes for the aged and infirm, I always try to see the face of Jesus in every person I meet. As this scripture says, I have met some angels along the way.

I pray to the Lord to give me a cheerful and generous spirit of hospitality to all new people that I meet. Will one of them be Him?

Revelation 3:16

So, because you are lukewarm, neither hot nor cold, I will vomit you out of my mouth.

As they say, this verse "separates the men from the boys." Every single one of us goes through periods when our spiritual life takes a backseat to worldly cares. It is during those periods when we may experience waning enthusiasm, a tepid relationship with God, and faith without zeal.

When I am drifting along, doing the absolute minimum to build the kingdom of God, the Lord grabs me by the lapels and tells me, "Listen up! Nothing is more aggravating to Me than your lukewarm attitude. You are like stale dishwater in My mouth. Change direction or I must spit you out onto the ground."

Wow! God is unequivocal about this, isn't He? Lukewarm is not permitted! I need to show zeal, heat, sparks—everything that demonstrates I am God's loyal, committed disciple. When malaise strikes my soul, may the Lord send me the graces of enthusiasm, resolve, and determination.

Romans 8:26–27

The Spirit, too, comes to the aid of our weakness; for we do not know how to pray as we ought, but the Spirit itself intercedes with inexpressible groanings. And the one who searches hearts knows what is the intention of the Spirit, because it intercedes for the holy ones according to God's will.

How many times have I felt arid in my prayer life? No level of concentration or request for God's grace seems to move my languid soul to communication with my Creator.

This scripture reminds me that the Holy Spirit is interceding for me with *inexpressible groanings*. I am told: "Don't worry, I will pray on your behalf. I know exactly what you need in your life. Whatever you require or seek, I will go to the Father and ask for you—no, not ask but *plead* your case."

This is deeply comforting when my personal prayer seems dry, empty, and ineffective. When that occurs, I can hear the divine groaning carrying my adoration, contrition, thanksgiving, and supplication to our Heavenly Father. For this, I offer the Spirit my love and gratitude.

John 21:25

There are also many other things that Jesus did, but if these were to be described individually, I do not think the whole world would contain the books that would be written.

All Christians love the words of scripture, especially those describing the works Jesus performed while on earth. Many people have become experts on the passages written about the life of our Lord and Savior. Yet, as we read in John, we are seeing only a fraction of what Jesus actually said and did during His brief three years of public ministry.

The writer says that the world could not contain all books which could have been written about what Jesus accomplished while on earth. What does that mean to us? I think it means that sacred scripture is very important to our understanding of what Jesus taught and did during His life. I think it also says that we must be open to other parts of His teaching that may have been passed on by word of mouth or accepted as true through the teaching and beliefs of his disciples.

Some may say, "No, written sacred scripture is all there is." I respectfully disagree. It was a relatively long time between the death of Jesus and the first writing of the accepted Gospels. How was common belief preserved during that time? I feel sure there was much in the way of traditional stories and beliefs passed from one believer to the next. While we cannot know exactly what happened in the early Church, there must have been much eyewitness testimony that was passed on orally.

I pray that the Lord gives me an open mind. There is much about Jesus I do not necessarily know because it was not committed to writing, but I feel sure it will all become clear to me when I reach my final goal of eternal life with God in heaven.

CONTRITION

Matthew 3:1–2

In those days John the Baptist appeared, preaching in the desert of Judea and saying, "Repent, for the kingdom of heaven is at hand!" It was said of him that the prophet Isaiah had spoken when he said:
"A voice of one crying out in the desert,
Prepare the way of the Lord,
Make straight his paths."

In my life, I have often acted as though the goal of my spirituality was to determine the minimum amount of good I must do to earn eternal life. I am ashamed of that, but it is the truth.

One of the New Testament's central themes is repentance. Scripture tells us over and over that we must change our lives radically—that is, repent. We can't just put a coat of new paint over the grime and call it good. We are told to truly change, to repent of our past sins and head in a new direction.

Can you imagine how unpopular John the Baptist must have been? Nobody—including me—likes to be told, "Stop cruising in a comfort zone! Make a fresh start." Sometimes I think, *Lord, don't you ever let up on me?* Yet, I can see, at my age, that the kingdom is at hand. I don't have time to quibble with God over what constitutes repentance. I must humbly accept that the time has come for a complete repentance in my life, and ask the Lord for help.

Matthew 6:20–21

Store up treasures in heaven, where neither moth nor decay destroys, nor thieves break in and steal. For where your treasure is, there also will your heart be.

> I know I spend too much time checking my bank balance, investments, and overall financial condition. I rationalize that I cannot earn it again, and therefore I must carefully preserve my wealth for future needs. Yet, I have had friends die suddenly; one moment, their riches were important to them, the next, meaningless.
>
> We are bombarded with materialism. "Money is a major source of happiness," we hear. "So acquire, invest, and save to build your treasure." What a false god this can be! My entire lifespan takes place in a wink... At the end, only one thing matters: have I been faithful to my God and the path He has laid out for me? Will I have riches stored up in heaven? Or, will they be carefully hoarded riches here on earth, that decay along with my human flesh?
>
> Most important is that my heart be in the right place.

Matthew 12:30

Whoever is not with me is against me, and whoever does not gather with me scatters.

> I am daily challenged with this passage's crystal clarity. I cannot be lukewarm or halfhearted about my commitment. There is no equivocation in this verse. I am not permitted to be "kind of" a follower. No "mostly" or "sort of" is acceptable. Like the captain leading his company into battle, Jesus turns, looks into my eyes and says, "Are you with me—totally?"
>
> Oh, how I want to be!!! But my weak human spirit tries to convince me otherwise. The dark angel residing

inside me says, "You can't be expected to do it all yourself. Do what you can but don't worry if you can't give one hundred percent. No one is expected to do that!"

Confronted with all or nothing, I must heed this call no matter how difficult or unnerving it may be. I must accept all God's love and all His challenges as well. I ask the Lord to help me in my weakness.

Matthew 18:21–22

Then Peter approaching asked him, "Lord, if my brother sins against me, how often must I forgive him? As many as seven times?" Jesus answered, "I say to you, not seven times but seventy-seven times."

I have been told that the number seven and multiples of it represented virtual infinity in Jesus' time. So, I think this passages calls me to forgive, forgive, and then forgive some more.

Forgiveness is not something I do well or easily. A slight insult, a harsh word, or a mean-spirited exchange can leave me fuming and in no mood to forgive anyone. But Jesus tells me to get over it. He says to me, "Forgive that person now and if he does it again, shrug it off and forgive him again. And keep doing just that until I tell you to stop." He must have some idea how hard that is for me. (Of course, Jesus knows but that's not the point; forgiveness is the point).

In the Lord's Prayer I say, "Forgive us our trespasses as we forgive others." I am asking God to be as forgiving to me as I am to others. I can only throw myself on God's infinite mercy and hope He is patient with my weak, flawed human nature, which must struggle so much to grant forgiveness to others.

My prayer is, as always, "I will try to do as You say, Lord, but I cannot do it without Your graces."

Matthew 26:39

My Father, if it is possible, let this cup pass from me; yet, not as I will, but as you will.

Jesus, fully divine and fully human, knew exactly what Friday would bring. He knew that his physical body would have to endure unspeakable agony, pain, suffering, and humiliation. His dear human nature must have trembled to think about what would happen to Him. And so, He made a reasonable cry for help.

"Father, can you let me escape this cup?" Yet His obedience and integrity required Him to add, "Not as I will, Father, but as You will."

There is no more perfect act of sacrifice for our sins. I so often fall short in similar situations. I want God to let me off the hook and not make me suffer indignity or pain. I want my will to prevail, not God's. Yet, I know that is not what I am called to do. I must learn to end all my prayers of pleading by also saying, "I want this, Lord, but I accept whatever Your will is in this situation."

This is hard for me to do, and I ask the Lord to help me.

Mark 9:41

Anyone who gives you a cup of water to drink because you belong to Christ, amen, I say to you, will surely not lose his reward.

I think this passage is different from what we hear in Matthew 25: ""I was thirsty and you gave me to drink." This verse specifically speaks about giving aid to a fellow Christian. I believe "a cup of water" is an allegory for aid, assistance, love and care given to someone who is a member of Christ's church.

It does not say, however, that those unwilling to give the same assistance to a non-Christian will be punished. I do feel called to a special relationship with my fellow religionists much as I would with any family member. Yet this does not mean that I deny the same love and care to a Muslim, Buddhist, Jew, or atheist. The Lord does not ask us to take a roll call before offering our hand to any person.

Still, in the course of my daily life, my contacts are usually Christians. It is comforting for me to hear from Jesus that any help I offer them is noted by God and helps me achieve my final, eternal reward. I know I can't earn my way into heaven by my actions. Even my next breath, and my existence, are gifts from God. But a passage like this does give me great hope as I contemplate my final judgment, when I shall meet my God face-to-face.

Luke 6:37

Stop judging and you will not be judged. Stop condemning and you will not be condemned. Forgive and you will be forgiven.

When I read this, my first thought is always the same: Why must God single me out so clearly in scripture?

I am ashamed to admit that judging, condemning, and not forgiving others are some of my most intransigent character traits. No matter what, God's commandment to love my neighbor always seems to run into a brick wall of judgment. At least, through the grace of God, I am permitted to see my sinfulness with clarity.

I revisit this verse frequently, each time begging the Lord to patch and repair my broken spirit so I commit these sins no more. I learned long ago that I cannot improve alone. Only through an outpouring of God's grace will I be able to mend my soul.

The Lord is so patient with me, and His help is always available.

Luke 23:34

Then Jesus said, "Father, forgive them, they know not what they do."

It seems incredible: Jesus, hanging from the cross and in the final minutes of His human, earthly life, asks His Father to forgive those who have brutally and relentlessly mutilated His body. In a final act of love, He says to His Father, "They wouldn't have done this to Me if they really understood who I am. Be gentle with them, Father, since they are just weak humans who have made a serious mistake in judgment."

Can you imagine yourself, in similar circumstances, doing what our crucified Savior did? I could never be so generous. The slightest wrong can leave me angry and vengeful.

Each time I say the Lord's Prayer I repeat the words, "Forgive us our trespasses as we forgive those who trespass against us." I wonder if I really mean this, sometimes, or if the words just come out of my mouth in a jumble of memorized prayer? I can only throw myself on the Lord's mercy and ask for His gentle understanding of my flawed nature.

I want to be like Him, but some of the standards He have set require more than I am able to give. Only His grace can save.

Acts 2:32

God raised this Jesus; of this we are all witnesses.

Even today, many scoff at the resurrection of Jesus. "It was not real," they say. "More likely it was a case of resuscitation rather than resurrection. In any event, this so-called resurrection was just a myth created by zealots to establish their own power and control the superstitious masses." Usually these words are snorted out, skeptically.

How sad that many believe this. Their unbelief is as old as Jesus' human death. Back then, their leaders were desperate to have this "Jesus thing" just go away. A dead and discredited Jesus would have restored power and prestige to those who had always been considered the leaders. If this new cult thrived, who could say how it might disrupt the establishment?

Peter, at the first Pentecost, boldly proclaimed that he and the other apostles and disciples were witnesses to Jesus' resurrection. How I wish I had been an actual witness, too! As Jesus said to Thomas, "Blessed are those who do not see but still believe." Through this gift of faith I believe unconditionally in the Lord's resurrection. Without this conviction, all other faith in Jesus crumbles, too.

Acts 15:22

It is necessary for us to undergo many hardships to enter the kingdom of God.

Life is not called a "vale of tears" for nothing. Each one of us experiences loss, heartache, illness, and difficulty in our day-to-day journey. Why? If we are living decent lives and doing our best to answer the Lord's call to love God and our neighbor, why must we suffer these hardships? Is God being vengeful for our past transgressions?

Of course not. God loves each of us unconditionally and wants what is best for us. But we do have free will and, thankfully, our lives are not predestined. When bad things overtake us, and make our life sad, difficult, and painful, the fault is not with God. Negative events are part of the human condition.

We must accept them for what they are. Like metal tempered in fire, we are likewise strengthened by tough times. I ask the Lord to help me keep my perspective when events in my life turn sour. We must trust Him to show us how to use difficult times to embrace Him more completely, and to continue to love us when we are most discouraged and disheartened.

Romans 7:19

For I do not do the good I want, but I do the evil I do not want.

What scripture sums up my life better than this? Riding pious waves of intense prayer and feeling good about my spiritual life, I find myself violently knocked to the ground just like Saul on the road to Damascus.

I sincerely want to "do good," but fail through my weakness. I am uncompromising about "avoiding evil," yet sin at the first sign of temptation. My only hope is in the great love and infinite forgiveness that God unceasingly offers to fragile human beings like me.

Ephesians 5:25

Husbands, love your wives; even as Christ loved the church and handed himself over for her…

At this writing, I have been married to my wife for over 51 years. I wish I had always followed the words of this verse. Like most (all?) marriages, ours has had its ups and downs.

Without trying to be noble, I can say that most of our difficulties have been caused by my failure to love as this passage suggests. My wonderful spouse has always done her best; at times, I have not. Regardless, this scripture gives me an ideal to strive for. I am told to love my wife in the same way Christ loves those who make up His church.

More than love is required to live out Jesus' example. Sacrifice is also required. He willingly handed Himself over, thus providing a seed of growth for His church. For the times I have failed to love my wife as I ought, I ask for the Lord's mercy and forgiveness. I already know that she has forgiven me many times. I pray He is as full of love and pardon as my wife has been over these many years of marriage.

Colossians 3:13–14

...as the Lord has forgiven you, so must you also do. And over all these, put on love.

It seems that whatever page I read in the Bible tells me that I have been forgiven and must do the same for others. It says that being a disciple of Christ is being joyful, uplifting—and kind of easy.

As for me, I do not grant forgiveness to others easily, cheerfully, or swiftly. I know that God has absolved me with His abundant mercy more times than I wish to count. When I sin against Him or against my neighbor, I run to the Almighty begging for mercy and pardon. I am not so generous myself. Why is it so hard for me to be equally forgiving of people who have offended me? I find myself face-to-face with one of my greatest failings.

I ask the Lord to patch up my soul and help me emulate His loving mercy and forgiveness. I wish to pardon other, and as scripture says, above all else put on love. This is so hard for me to do, and I pray for divine assistance.

Matthew 19:23 and Luke 18:24–25

Then Jesus said to his disciples, "Amen, I say to you, it will be hard for one who is rich to enter the kingdom of heaven."

How hard it is for those who have wealth to enter the kingdom of God! For it is easier for a camel to pass through the eye of a needle than for a rich person to enter the kingdom of God.

These two passages from Matthew and Luke can cause great spiritual concern for anyone who has accumulated wealth during their lifetime.

The old saying, "Money is the root of all evil," seems especially pertinent today. We can find countless vivid examples of greed, outrageous salaries, and obsessive acquisition of wealth for wealth's sake. On the other hand, we often hear of enormously generous philanthropy by some who enjoyed huge success in business.

But what of those who have been fortunate enough to accumulate a modest estate—one that will see them through old age and leave something for their heirs and for charity? Even if these estates are not extravagant, only a very small percentage of the total population is so fortunate.

I believe the modestly wealthy can enter heaven. Perhaps I am rationalizing, since I have been able to create a comfortable estate for my family. Am I kidding myself? Would it be easier for me to pass through the eye of a needle?

I would like to think Jesus means that his followers shouldn't be *too* focused on wealth. I believe He is telling me that a compulsive attachment to money is the problem, not the money itself. He wants to know: Do I give generously and anonymously to charity and to those less fortunate? Is my first thought, "What I can do to help others with my treasure?" Or is it, "What I can do to increase it?"

I have been told that "the eye of the needle" is a gate into the City of Jerusalem. In order to enter through this portal, a person must totally unload his camel of all his possessions so that the animal will fit through. Perhaps this is a metaphor for someone, like me, who is trying to maintain a healthy detachment from material wealth so that I can pass into heaven.

I give thanks to God for the wonderful, productive life He has permitted me to lead. I ask that I be given the grace of detachment from worldly things, and pray that He will help me use my wealth to improve the lives of others.

Matthew 25:31–46

The Judgment of the Nations.
(For complete scripture text, see endnotes).

I believe this is one of the most significant passages in the New Testament. It sums up everything one must do in this earthly life to prepare for never-ending happiness in the afterlife.

Jesus tells the story about the end of the world. All people are assembled and divided into two groups. The Son of Man will say to one group, "Come, you blessed of my Father. Inherit the kingdom prepared for you from the foundation of the world." Then the Lord will tell them what they did to gain this reward. He tells them they gave Him something to eat when He was hungry, they provided Him something to drink when He was thirsty, that they welcomed Him when He was a stranger and gave Him clothes when He had none.

These folks will answer, "Lord, when did we see You hungry, thirsty, a stranger or naked?" Then comes the punch line: "Whatever you did for one of My least brothers and sisters, you did for Me."

To the other group, He says, "Depart from me, you accursed, into eternal fire prepared for the devil." They cannot understand their fateful sentence. So the Lord tells them, "You didn't feed Me when I was hungry, you didn't quench My thirst, you never greeted Me when I was a stranger or clothed Me when I was naked." The people say, "Lord when did we see You hungry, thirsty, a stranger or naked?" Now the second punch line: "What you did *not* do for one of these least ones, you did *not* do for Me." The story concludes with the righteous people going off to a life of eternal happiness while the others are sent to eternal punishment.

In my surroundings I don't often see people who are actually hungry or thirsty. Did the Lord mean something else? Perhaps I come across people who are hungry and thirsty for the Word of God or justice or fair dealings from their employers. What have I done to assist them? I see strangers every day. Am I doing what I can to make them feel less lonely, isolated, or anxious about their environment?

There aren't too many naked people in my neighborhood, either. But there are lots of people living without safe shelter who must curl up in some rags in a doorway to sleep. What am I doing to assist them? It's strange. None of the people I mentioned appear anything like I expect Jesus to look. Most of the people who need my help are probably unkempt, dirty, and don't smell very nice, either. Frankly, it would be a lot easier to turn away when I meet them. They are so unlike me!

Mental illness and drug or alcohol addiction afflicts so many of them. Are they violent? Rational? If I get too close, am I putting myself in physical danger? Just when I am close to being revolted, I hear this tiny voice saying to me, "Whatever you do to these, my least ones, you do to Me." How can I turn my back? Jesus has given me a clear set of ground rules for how my life must be lived if I want a reward of eternal happiness. In my weakness I want to say, "Let someone else take care of these people." But that tiny voice keeps coming back again and again.

I pray for the Lord to help me in my weakness. I do want to care for Him, and I need Him to show me how to care for His least ones.

Matthew 27:46

Jesus cried out in a loud voice, "Eli, Eli, lema sabachthani?" which means, "My God, my God, why have you forsaken me?"

Think about your own life. Have you felt abandoned or forsaken by God? Was there ever a time when you could not find God no matter where or how hard you looked?

I have experienced this feeling several times. The first time was when I learned my dear sister, Ruth, was terminally ill. This just cannot be so, I thought! She is so accomplished, so loving, a good mother and thoughtful to my wife and me. "My God, my God, why have You forsaken me?"

The next time was in a doctor's office as he explained to me that I had an aggressive form of cancer. Why me? Where was my God when I needed Him? I thought, "My God, my God, why have You forsaken me?"

Then, after cancer surgery, I was called back to the doctor's office to hear that the operation had not been successful. Now, I must undergo an extensive series of powerful radiation treatments in hope of killing most of the remaining cancer cells floating in my abdomen. I thought, "My God, my God, why have You forsaken me?"

After the radiation treatments, the doctors felt that this approach had been successful, at least for the time being. Unfortunately, they told me, such high doses of radiation had been used that it probably barbecued most of my pelvic organs. You cannot expect to have a normal life from here on, they said. I thought, "My God, my God, why have You forsaken me?"

By the grace of God, I learned that God the Father did not abandon or forsake Jesus on the cross of Calvary. And my God has never forsaken me, either. To my clouded mind, it may seem that God is not nearby to help me in times of trial, and I feel alone, afraid, and without trust. But He is always at my side; I just may be looking for Him in the wrong places.

Luke 6:27–28

But to you who hear I say, love your enemies, bless those who curse you, pray for those who mistreat you.

I believe that God never gives us a burden we cannot handle. When I read these two verses I ask, "How can I possibly live out this scripture in my life? Tell me, Lord, how do I love my enemies? How do I bless those who curse me? How do I pray for those who mistreat me?"

My human makeup finds each of these commands all but impossible to deal with. I truly want to do what He asks of me, but I do not know how to cope with the request. What does it mean to love my enemies? Must I treat them exactly as I would my dearest loved ones? Does He really want me to pray for those who mistreat me? I do so, but I'm afraid my prayers are half-hearted and insincere.

My plea to the Lord is that he will show me how to fulfill His commands. My weak human spirit is much too limited to answer this request on my own.

Luke 6:41

Why do you notice the splinter in your brother's eye, but do not perceive the wooden beam in your own?

I have a number of traits that must be disagreeable to others. I have a well-honed ability to spot flaws in the way others conduct their lives. I frequently catch myself saying to friends, family, neighbors, even strangers, "You should do that differently," or perhaps, "You shouldn't be doing that at all."

I often wonder why I think that I have been appointed the boss over all these other people. Of course, upon reflection I know that I am not their boss and I should refrain from telling them all the things they should, and shouldn't, be doing. Yet it is not so easy to see my own failings.

This passage speaks directly to a weakness that I must overcome. How can I do that? Only by turning to God, and contritely seeking His graces and mercy. I ask that He helps me get my own house in perfect order before I begin dishing out advice to those around me.

Luke 15:7

I tell you ... there will be more joy in heaven over one sinner who repents than over ninety-nine righteous people who have no need of repentance.

Everyone, especially we sinners, should feel consoled by this verse. The Triune God, and all the angels and saints let out a mighty roar of thanks and praise, when one person repents his or her sins and returns to life of perpetual grace.

I am truly loved and looked after by my Lord. Even in my sinfulness, the Creator is eager to forgive me and unceasingly reaches out to me with the graces of repentance and reconciliation. Yes, all of us share in God's unconditional love. But somehow, the repentant sinner becomes a "first among equals."

When I have foolishly broken my relationship with God through my own willfulness and pride, He pours out grace so I will repent and return to His love. There is too much sinfulness in my life, and I ask the Lord for the strength to repent daily.

Acts 3:19

Repent, therefore, and be converted, that your sins may be wiped away.

Again and again, scripture calls me to repentance and conversion. But repentance from what? From a life lived ignobly, full of self-indulgence and indifference to others?

Some believe this passage refers to repentance from the seven deadly sins. Perhaps, but in my opinion, it isn't exclusive. Great public sins certainly calls for repentance, but so do the minor offenses we all commit daily—failures to turn my life over to God; to care for my neighbor; to step forward proclaiming my faith. I also must repent for always taking the path that looks easiest and least uncomfortable.

I pray to the Lord to keep me from becoming lukewarm or wishy-washy, and to lend me the grace to repent and convert my life. By repenting to the best of my spiritual ability, I trust that He will wipe away my sins.

Acts 17:30

God has overlooked the times of ignorance, but now he demands that all people everywhere repent.

God has been incredibly patient with mankind in general and with each of us individually. Consider what must register in God's divine spirit as He watches us thrash around, bound up in our weak and sinful nature committing stupid acts. Think of it: flying planes into buildings, letting children starve, cheating poor workers of wages and trashing the environment for greedy gain. I can picture God shaking His head and saying to Himself, "What is it going to take to get these folks to turn away from egregious sin?"

Time and time again, God has overlooked our failings but, as this passage says, patience only goes so far, even with God. "Now," He says to me, "you must change your ways and develop a sense of true repentance. I am not phrasing this as a suggestion; I demand that you do it!"

And I must answer, "OK, Lord, I hear you—I will do my best to get back on the right track, to repent of my past sinfulness and change the direction of my life." I thank you Him for being so patient with me in the past. Please remember that my good intentions often break down under the weight of human frailty. I know You love me and will continue to exercise Your patience with me even when I fail again. Your abundant mercy is a great and wonderful blessing to me.

Romans 12:4–5

For as in one body we have many parts, and all the parts do not have the same function, so we, though many, are one body in Christ and parts of one another.

Few scriptural passages provide more instruction than these do about living together and getting along.

Think of the complex human body. Externally we have eyes, ears, noses, mouths, necks, shoulders, arms, hands, legs, knees, and feet all covered with the largest human organ, skin. Inside there is a brain, heart, lungs, liver, kidneys, stomach, intestines, bladder, and a bunch of other things, too. This miraculous system called the human body operates because each of its parts and sub-systems take care of different needed functions.

This is the perfect metaphor for all of us humans living, working, and acting together. Every one of us is a member of Christ's body and therefore contiguous with one another—whether we like it or not.

We need to understand the implications of being members of the Body of Christ. Think of the time you got a paper cut on the tip of your finger. The pain shot up your arm, registered in your brain, forced your mouth to say, "Ouch," and made your whole body uncomfortable for a moment. And so it is with the Body of Christ. As John Donne wrote, "No man is an island unto himself."

The concept of the Body of Christ tells us that when one person is hurting or lost or leading a sinful life away from God's love, then we are *all* affected in some way. This profound idea is worth a lot of thought and prayer. What does it mean to *me* to be connected to my fellow human beings? Does it imply that I must work to establish different relationships than I have considered in the past? This requires heavy-duty thought and prayer.

I pray for the grace I need to properly understand my role as a member of the Body of Christ.

Proverbs 13:3

He who guards his mouth protects his life; to open wide one's lips brings downfall.

Well, isn't *that* the truth! Stop and think about how much trouble we can get into with our mouth. Why is it that we enjoy gossip, juicy rumors, snide comments about others, ribald and immoral stories, and unfair verbal characterizations about people's actions? Would you agree that our mouths cause us—and others—more problems than just about any other organ? Why can't we just learn to *shut up?*

We would all be well advised to follow the old bromide, "If you can't say something nice, don't say anything at all." But we just can't seem to help ourselves. We love to have the last word, win the argument or "one up" our verbal adversary. Lord, save us from our mouths!

I pray to Him to teach me to dip every word I speak in honey and in truth. To show me how much my unkind words can wound another person. To let me always be kind in what I say and gentle in how I say it. I need help to button my lip.

Philippians 2:14

Do everything without grumbling or questioning.

Lord, I'm sure You have a great sense of humor but You have got to be kidding on this one, right? To ask me to do everything I am supposed to without grumbling—even a little—seems above and beyond the call of duty. Haven't you seen the bumper sticker, "Question Authority?"

Well, assuming the Lord is not pulling my leg, I will certainly try. He is telling me that I need to accept what comes my way in life and not complain too much. I pray each day, "Thy will be done," meaning I should acknowledge that His will may not always be my will.

The Lord advises us to be thankful for all things and not complain or question. With a merciful, just, and loving God to trust, what have we got to whine about? Replacing our complaints with thanks, however, is not easy thing for many of us—certainly me—to do, so let us seek His blessings and grace to fulfill His commandment.

Colossians 2:8

See to it that no one captivate you with an empty, seductive philosophy according to human tradition, according to the elemental powers of the world and not according to Christ.

I am stunned by the relentless assaults by secular, anti-God elements on traditional spiritual values and on those who try to live by them. It would be easy if the attacks created an obvious "good guy–bad guy," but it doesn't seem to work that way in real life.

The worldly blandishments tend to be so seductive, attractive, and logical that the "good guys" are painted as a marginalized, hateful, loony group who are out of touch with the modern world's mores. The worst part? I'm afraid the "bad guys" are winning this social argument.

What lesson can we learn from this? I see that my prayers must become more intense and focused. I cannot withstand this avalanche of secularism with my own will. Those who would cut me off from God are much too clever for me. As the writer says, I am pitted against "the elemental powers of the world."

I pray that the Lord stands in front of me and protects me from the violence the world would inflict upon me. May he keep me safe in His love.

1 Timothy 1:14b

Christ Jesus came into the world to save sinners. Of these I am the foremost.

St. Paul was always instructing his friends, including Timothy. I think all Christian believers will stipulate that the first sentence in this verse is an essential credo among Christians.

The second sentence is the one I question. Paul unashamedly professes that he is the foremost of all sinners. Hey, how about me? Paul may have thought that his murderous purges against Jesus' followers qualified him as the first among all sinners. Yet I am not shy about telling you that I have also led a life full of stupid mistakes, poor choices, unfulfilled promises, and other garden-variety sins. I am not seeking the title of "First Among All Sinners," but it just seems to me that there is way too much sin in my life.

When I go to church, I often visualize a large neon sign on top of the building that says, "Sinners Welcome!" The image always makes me feel better. My great hope is in the infinite mercy of God Almighty. May that mercy, patience, and love sustain me.

Hebrews 12:7

Endure your trials as discipline; God treats you as (children). For what (child) is there whom the father does not discipline?

As the father of six children, I can identify with this passage. I love each of my six kids, but along the road to adulthood, none of them escaped some form of discipline from their mother or me.

Some punishment was harsh because we decided that a very important lesson needed to be learned. Other controls were gentle, when only a small course correction was required.

As God's children, we are in the same situation. In this verse we hear that life's trials should be considered the Father's loving discipline in our lives. The only problem is that none of us wants to be disciplined. It always hurts physically or emotionally and most often restricts our freedoms.

My job is to keep the correct mindset when I encounter trials. I can grouse and complain about my fate or I can try to accept the hard times I am experiencing as God's way of getting my attention.

As always, I pray for the strength and courage to learn from the difficulties. I ask to be shown each day how much He loves me, even when I face struggles that seem too much to bear.

1 Peter 1:24–25

All flesh is like grass, and all its glory like the flower of the field; the grass withers, and the flower wilts but the word of the Lord remains forever.

I have lived in Oregon for almost twenty years. Having seen much of the rest of the world, I can tell you that Oregon is one of the most beautiful places on earth. While the temperature is relatively mild, the western Willamette

Valley experiences all four seasons of the year. That means our gray, wet, and sometimes cold winter is followed by a gorgeous spring bringing an explosion of colorful flowers, leafed-out trees, and grasses of every kind. We enjoy a wonderful, warm summer watching trees produce fruit, spring flowers giving way to summer varieties, while other vegetation matures and ripens in the heat. Finally, the crisp days of autumn announce the end of the flowers and fruit, and the leaves of the deciduous trees take on brilliant fall hues. Then, the rains return, winter settles in, and all of us wait for spring again.

How many more times will I be blessed to see this cycle? This scripture verse uses a similar cycle to explain the span of each person's life. In the normal course, we grow out of childhood into adulthood, middle age, and finally old age. Like the beautiful flowers and grasses, we are vibrant, strong, and full of life for a time, but slowly begin to fade and wilt as we reach the end of our lives. As the writer so aptly says, the eternal word of God endures forever even though each of us leaves this human life for a place that is everlasting.

I pray that the Lord will help me understand that my human existence is but a short time compared to eternity. May I also see that His words are timeless. I pray that His love, mercy, and unbounded care will continue to touch the hearts and souls of all the loved ones who will live on after me; and that the Lord will protect them as He has so generously cared for me.

1 John 2:3

The way we may be sure that we know him is to keep his commandments.

Many of us profess to be disciples of Jesus Christ and are card-carrying members of the Christian church. Since all of us are human beings, there are inevitably many sinners among these members. Some who profess Christianity don't keep God's commandments—some of us talk a good game, but we don't always walk the talk.

That's OK. Even a sinner can find reconciliation and forgiveness through the grace of God. Yet God still expects us to profess our belief in Him and also to keep His commandments.

He says to me during my prayer time, "How else will I truly know that you love me? Show Me by doing what I have asked you to do." I say that I will try to do my best.

The Lord, more than anyone, knows I am a sinner. I fall much too often. I pray for him to help me get up, brush myself off, and keep slogging toward the Promised Land. I pray that the Lord be merciful to me, an abject sinner.

Matthew 11:28–30

Come to me, all you who labor and are burdened, and I will give you rest. Take my yoke upon you and learn from me, for I am meek and humble of heart; and you will find rest for yourselves. For my yoke is easy and my burden light.

You have seen the picture—two oxen working together under a wooden yoke mounted over their shoulders as they pull a plow, furrow, or other heavy tool.

I sometimes find myself mightily burdened by the difficulties of life. I am exhausted from fighting my battles against materialism, secularism, and the cares of daily toil. Pulling this plow alone is hard work indeed, and I am sore tired. But Jesus says to me, "Stop worrying; you don't have to take care of everything by yourself. You and I will be yoked together to handle whatever burden is sent your way. When I am there, standing side-by-side with you, the burdens you bear will be much lighter. Just ask Me and I will be happy to help."

His words convince me that there is nothing I can't handle if I just turn to Him for help. With Him in the yoke next to me, I can deal with anything.

Deuteronomy 4:2

In your observance of the commandments of the Lord, Your God, which I enjoin upon you, you shall not add to what I command nor subtract from it.

Sometimes I feel a desire to personally pick the commandments that are convenient for me to follow and ignore the ones I don't like. God tells me this is a no-no. Equally unacceptable is the temptation to add to the requirements, especially when it might apply to others—but not me. He has sent sufficient instructions for living a pious life. It is not necessary for us to add to the Lord's statutes nor is it permitted for us to subtract from them.

It is human nature to try and bend the rules to make them fit our situations better. I entreat the Lord to teach me compliance. He has shown me the path to salvation, and I hope He will also give me the grace to accept the path He have set out for us, the brothers and sisters in the Body of Christ.

Luke 6:31

Do to others as you would have them do to you.

This is the Golden Rule that we all learned in our youth. It is a simple way to deal with others, simply put.

It has been said that if all humankind truly followed this rule we would be peace on earth. And yet, as I observe my home, my community, my state, my nation—even the whole world—I see conflict, disputes, and wars because people refuse to treat others as they themselves want to be treated. At the expense of others, I find myself pushing to the head of a line, demanding superior position on the roads and highways, wanting the better seat at a concert, insisting that I receive service before others. All that is asked of me is to treat others with the same fairness I want for myself.

Why is this so hard for me to do? What flaw in my soul demands the best portion? I might not be able to end all world conflicts, but I could make a difference in my own limited environment.

I pray that the Lord sends me His help, so that I may see every opportunity to apply His rule in the places I live, work, and recreate. May He give me the grace to consistently live by His word in my own life. It could make a world of difference.

Luke 12:15

Take care to guard against all greed, for though one may be rich, one's life does not consist of possessions.

I need to be careful about this passage. I have been most fortunate in my life. Through hard work, luck, and the grace of God, I have been able to accumulate a modest fortune.

While I have tried to keep my wealth (such as it is) in perspective, there have been more times than I like to admit when I've been consumed by the chance to hit a financial home run. I have found myself plotting and scheming about ways to leverage some opportunity into a big "pay day" for me. I have never considered doing anything that was illegal, immoral, or would hurt someone else. But I have wavered sometimes about what really was important to me in life.

Sad to say, there have been times when I may have thought my life consisted of possessions. Greed instead of God possessed my spirit, at least for a while. I must pray in times of temptation, when earthly possessions look like the most important thing in my life, for the Lord to send His graces and help me remember the heavenly prize.

Luke 15:11–32

The parable of the Prodigal Son.
(For complete scripture text, see endnotes).

This beautiful story is full of interesting sub-plots. First, a younger son asks his father to divide the estate and give him his share—now. Reading between the lines, you can sense that the father knows this is a mistake, but he fulfills his young son's greedy request anyway.

The son quickly squanders his new riches in a self-indulgent lifestyle. The young man then pays a terrible price for his dissolute life, and he returns home to his father with a carefully rehearsed but sincere plea for forgiveness.

The father's compassionate and loving response to his wayward son is beautiful and somewhat unexpected. The older son shows his bitter displeasure that his younger brother is getting off "scot-free." The father is pleads with him to join him in forgiveness and rejoicing because the young son has returned.

We don't know whether or not the father's plea was effective. This story is about how God permits us to exercise our own free will even when we make bad choices. We also learn about the four steps leading to true reconciliation—contrition, conversion, confession, and celebration—and how they apply to our own daily life. The story also reinforces how happy our God is when we do repent of our sins and return to a life of grace.

I even relate to the anger of the older son. Sometimes I think people who may have offended me get off way too easy. How come they're so lucky, I ask myself?

I also see myself in the prodigal son, especially the part about poor choices followed by "coming to my senses at last," which led to contrition and conversion. When I finally turned to God again, embarrassed by my sinfulness, I found a merciful, forgiving Lord who loves me unconditionally even before I confess my sins. My soul celebrates at having been forgiven, and there is celebration in heaven for my repentance.

May the Lord help me always turn away from my sinful mistakes and return to His abundant love. When I meet Him face-to-face at the end of my earthly life, I hope He will treat me the same way the father in this story treated his wayward son.

Acts 2:28

You have made known to me the paths of life; you will fill me with joy in your presence.

Life's journey takes us along diverse pathways. Every person encounters different roads throughout his or her stay on this earth. Some lanes are strewn with rocks, potholes, and other obstacles.

Walking down those trails can cause me pain, heartache, and discouragement. At other times, I tread on smooth paths bathed in bright sunshine and bordered with gorgeous flowers. In other words, my life, like all others, is a series of ups and downs.

In good times and in bad, the Lord makes known to me the paths I should follow. Because I am human and weak, I can easily miss the signs He has posted for me; if I do not pay attention, it is simple to take a wrong turn or wind up on a road leading to nowhere. When I follow His directions, I believe I will be filled with much joy because I am walking in His presence.

I ask the Lord Jesus to please continue to send me up-to-date maps that lead me on His pathways.

Acts 7:60

Then he (Stephen) fell to his knees and cried out in a loud voice, "Lord, do not hold this sin against them;" and when he had said this, he fell asleep.

I am fascinated with Stephen. Appointed in the early days of the church as a deacon, his perceived duties were to assist the apostles in the daily chores of caring for people in the church who needed help.

He was probably a young man, certainly not well educated or particularly well versed in Jewish scripture. Yet, he immediately became one of the chief apologists for The Way, confounding the elders and scribes with his compelling arguments on behalf of Jesus, the crucified and resurrected Messiah. His persuasive presentations infuriated those in power. Under the supervision of Saul, Stephen was stoned to death.

While dying he pleaded with the Lord to forgive his murderers. Could I possibly be so forgiving in the same situation? I nurse grudges for even the slightest perceived offense. This scripture reminds me how far I have to go in my own spiritual life, and that abundant graces from God are needed.

Romans 6:23

For the wages of sin is death, but the gift of God is eternal life in Christ Jesus our Lord.

I am often reminded that my spiritual life is full of stark choices. I hear in this passage that the payoff for turning my back on God is death for my immortal soul. Should I actually die while carrying the stain of a serious sin on my spirit, I surely risk eternal damnation. That sobering thought should be enough to keep me on the straight and narrow. But it hasn't always.

I rationalize: God is all-merciful; He could never condemn me to everlasting hellfire. I forget that He is also all-just. He has given me free will. Should I make horrendous and sinful choices, He will let me do so and respect my decisions. "If you do not love Me and turn your back," He says, "I will let you do so—but you must pay the consequences because I am a just God."

On the other hand, God sent His only begotten Son to open the gates of heaven to all people. I can choose an eternity of heavenly bliss in God's presence if I wish.

I pray that God sends strength as I guard against offending Him by my thoughts, words, and actions. May he remind me always that earthly life is but a blink of time, and eternity is forever. I want to spend it with Him.

Tobit 3:3

*And now, O Lord, may **Y**ou be mindful of me, and look with favor upon me. Punish me not for my sins nor for my inadvertent offenses, nor for those of my fathers.*

"Lord, can You see me? Can You hear my prayers? How am I doing?" Every once in a while, I feel the need to seek some feedback from God. Not that He ever answers me in words. But I do ask Him if He still loves me and is looking out for me—you know, the same way a child sometimes does with a parent. "Daddy, will you always love me, no matter what?"

Notice the plea to dismiss personal sins as "inadvertent offenses." I am seeking a "pass" on the sins I have committed, hoping that God is totally forgiving, merciful—and, perhaps, even myopic. The writer also seeks separation from any transgressions that might have been committed by ancestors. "Don't hold their sins against me, Lord—I had nothing to do with those faults."

This little verse charms me with the simplicity of its plea to God. "I don't want You to forget *me*, Lord, but I *do want* You to forget my sins and the sins of my fathers." I'm sure God is quite understanding, even when my request seems to want it both ways.

I hope the Lord will be gentle with me when my prayers to Him are less than profound.

1 Thessalonians 4:13

We do not want you to be unaware, brothers (and sisters), about those who have fallen asleep, so that you may not grieve like the rest, who have no hope.

I love the Roman Catholic tradition to pray for those who have died. We know our departed dear ones no longer experience any human suffering. Death releases each of us into the arms of our Heavenly Father.

We have great trust in God's infinite mercy and love for each of us—but we don't *really* know what it is like on the other side of the door leading to eternity. And so we pray earnestly, asking that those who have died be taken by Jesus to the Father's side in paradise. While I cannot have specific knowledge of the afterlife, I do have a great sense of hope. God has made many promises about the rewards I may expect in return for an earthly life dedicated to His service.

I will trust that the Lord is merciful to my departed loved ones, friends—and that he will be so to me at that moment I breathe my last human breath.

I pray now that Jesus will remind me to offer petitions for those who have gone before me as well for as myself. I rely upon His mercy—to them, to me, and to those who will follow me.

1 Thessalonians 5:22

Refrain from every kind of evil.

While the whole of God's creation is wonderful and glorious, the temptation to commit evil lurks around every corner. The devil is alive and well and seeks to capture all of us in his nets.

I believe it is not only a mistake to equate evil just with the seven deadly sins or great public iniquity, but that such a mistake is one of Satan's ploys. He says to us, "Don't worry, you would never be guilty of a *mortal* sin and God will easily forgive you the small mistakes you may make." How effortlessly we can then justify our small indulgences. After all, I am not a murderer, adulterer, nor do I beat my children. "Your sins are insignificant," the devil whispers, "so don't be so concerned when you commit them." This is a beguiling but thoroughly depraved message.

Gossip, envy, selfishness, love of material things, and many other "small" things can corrode our soul. I am called to avoid evil *in every form*.

I ask the Lord to help me be always on guard. Yes, my weak human nature may often trip and fall, but with His help I can get up again and resolve to shun evil in whatever form it is placed before me.

James 2:13

For the judgment is merciless to one who has not shown mercy; mercy triumphs over judgment.

Oh, this verse just terrifies me! As I have said elsewhere in this book, my judgment of others is highly developed; my mercy to others always seems to be grudging.

I selected this verse because it is so important for me to be reminded of this terrible flaw in my spiritual character. Perhaps if I read my own writing enough, I may start to get the message that a total conversion of my spirit is in order.

In the meantime, I beg the merciful Lord to continue shaping my moral disposition so that I can become more in accord with this verse from St. James. Without His constant help, I will be lost.

1 Peter 5:8

Be sober and vigilant. Your opponent the devil is prowling around like a roaring lion looking for someone to devour.

Most of us go about our daily business without seeing bogeymen in every shadow. It is hard for many to imagine that a real devil exists on this earth, an evil spirit who ensnares anyone he can.

And yet the writer says to us: "Be careful! Satan is really present and he will devour you in a minute, given the chance." When we examine medieval art, especially, we often observe grotesque representations of Satan and his evil spirits. Of course, he would never show himself to us that way. He comes to us in gentle words, simple little suggestions, and alluring ideas—all intended to suck us into his hellish vortex.

"Why don't you read that book?" he whispers. "It has some lurid parts but it will not harm you." Or he may say, "There is always more time; you can repair that little disagreement you have with God later on." Perhaps he says, "You have given long enough; it's time for you to indulge yourself now." He is charming, alluring, seemingly innocent—never roaring, grotesque, or filled with blackness. That is why he is so dangerous.

I have personally seen him too often and I am afraid of him and what he can do. He even went after Lord Jesus, and Jesus had to fight him off. I pray for Jesus' assistance when the devil enters my space, offering captivating ideas that can crush my soul. May He give me the grace to fend off Satan when I am most vulnerable.

THANKSGIVING

Matthew 25:29

For to everyone who has, more will be given and he will grow rich; but from the one who has not, even what he has will be taken away.

To me, this verse has nothing to do with money. I have always believed that these words mean I must use my God-given gifts to advance His kingdom on earth.

Nor do I see this proposal as a "zero sum" activity. If I use my gifts humbly and wisely, I can count on God to entrust me with even more—thus enriching my opportunity to serve Him. But that does not mean that I will be blessed with more gifts at the expense of someone else.

Some people are blessed with a talent or gift that they seem unable to use appropriately. I am glad it is not my duty to judge. I cannot worry what others do with their gift; I can only pray for them and ask for God's continued blessings on them. On the other hand, growing rich by receiving more of God's gifts can be a mixed blessing. If I am blessed with more, I will also be expected to do more. This becomes the perfect example of "being careful what you pray for."

I pray that whatever gifts the Lord bestows on me, He gives me the grace to use them in His Name.

Luke 4:13

When the devil had finished every temptation, he departed from [Jesus] for a time.

This passage is found in the story of the three temptations of Jesus, after his forty days of solitude in desert, prior to the beginning of his public ministry. When I read the story of the encounter between Jesus and the devil, I find it easy to interpret it as the bad guy taking his best shot at Jesus, failing to break Him, and then just leaving Him alone. But those three little words at the end of the verse, *for a time*, tell a different story.

Jesus was a man, and men are never free of temptation. We know that Jesus in His human nature "is like us in all things but sin." How comforting this is to me! I struggle with temptation all the time. So did Jesus. I get angry, sad, tired, frustrated, and hungry. So did Jesus. I need nutrition, exercise, sleep, and a bath. So did Jesus. When life seems difficult for me I can picture Jesus facing the same situations with His fully human nature.

I am grateful to the Lord for coming down to this earth as one of us. He has shown us that we can overcome much if only we emulate Him.

Luke 12:6–7

Are not five sparrows sold for two small coins? Yet not one of them has escaped the notice of God. Even the hairs of your head have all been counted. Do not be afraid. You are worth more than many sparrows.

I wish I knew more about birds. We have so many of them where we live. I like the hummingbirds best; their aerodynamics are almost unbelievable—a true miracle of God. I like the tiny yellow and black finches, too, who bathe and drink from the fountain in our garden. They are gorgeous little creatures, so busy and full of happy life.

But enough about ornithology. God tells that these little winged creatures are pretty insignificant in the overall scheme of things. Yet each and every one of them rates notice from our Creator.

What God is really saying to me is this: "I watch over all these little birds. Don't you understand that you're more important than they are? I know *everything* about you, even the number of hairs on your head. Have faith and trust in Me. Don't be afraid for the future. I am always looking out for you and your welfare."

I thank Him for these reassuring words. But trust is harder than it sounds. I ask also for the grace to put my trust in Him and to let me see how much unconditional love He offers in each moment.

Romans 5:19

For just as through the disobedience of one person the many were made sinners, so through the obedience of one the many will be made righteous.

Our original ancestor, Adam, committed the profound sin of disobedience to God. Because of that, all mankind who followed bore the stain of original sin. It left us with clouded intellects, weak natures, and bodies subject to death and decay. Yet it is useless to blame Adam and Eve for our plight today.

Who knows how any of us might have reacted given the same set of circumstances? If I were Adam and you were Eve, could we have committed the same sin? Most probably. The more important matter is what God has done to change our hopelessness into hope.

While we all were tainted by the sin of Adam, we have all been made righteous by the obedient son, Jesus, who took the form of a man and through His death and resurrection, reopened the gates of heaven for all mankind. How can I possibly show my gratitude for such a generous gift? Is it truly possible for us to understand what God has done for us? Even everlasting thanks is inadequate.

2 Samuel 22:28–29

You save lowly people, though on the lofty Your eyes look down. You are my lamp, O Lord! O my God, You brighten the darkness about me.

> I am attracted to this passage because it refers to my God as a lamp. In my business career, I was involved in several manufacturing companies that produced lamps and lighting fixtures—perhaps that is why I feel a special affinity to these words.
>
> I know the Lord looks out for the lowly and disdains those who think they are lofty. Most important, He acts as a light source to brighten my world. I am grateful to Him for illuminating everything in my universe with His dazzling light, and pray that he remains present to me so that I may always operate in the light.

2 Corinthians 9:6–7b

Consider this: whoever sows sparingly will also reap sparingly and whoever sows bountifully will also reap bountifully...for God loves a cheerful giver.

> So many institutions rely on voluntary financial support to survive and do their commendable work in the community. We are aware of organizations involved in the arts, civic-oriented activities, and charitable groups who could not exist without public contributions of volunteer time, special talents, and above all, money.
>
> Individual church congregations are a perfect example. With few exceptions, parishes exist on Sunday collections, a variety of fundraisers, and special campaigns to raise large amounts of money for needed repairs, new buildings,

etc. While sometimes appearing coercive, the techniques are necessary to raise money from the church members.

Decisions about the level of financial support can be agonizing for families. What about all the other money pressures we face? Mortgages, school costs, transportation, medical and dental care, food and clothing—these and other items make relentless demands on our limited incomes. People of goodwill are often perplexed and anguished over this request to give cheerfully.

What does scripture say? If I am sparing with my gifts, the gifts coming back to me will also be spare. Alternatively, if I am generous (perhaps more generous than I planned to be), the gifts returning to me will also be generous. I am clearly told that God loves a cheerful giver.

While not stated in these verses, I also believe the notion that we cannot be more generous than God. Yet none of these promises of return make my worldly decision any easier. I hear of those who tithe ten percent of their income to charity and don't feel a pinch. I want to always act on a celestial plane but often experience a lot of human, mundane pressure as well. I have to ask the Lord for help in giving what is appropriate for my circumstances and always doing so cheerfully.

Galatians 5:22–23

The fruit of the Spirit is love, joy, peace, patience, kindness, generosity, faithfulness, gentleness, self-control. Against such there is no law.

The fruits listed are luscious, tasty, and delicious. The Holy Spirit, dwelling inside each person, brings all these blessings to us. They are ours for the taking. But sometimes we find it hard to attain some or all of them and retain them in our soul.

Wouldn't it be wonderful if we could always feel a spirit of love, joy, peace, patience, kindness, generosity, faithfulness, gentleness, and self-control in the core of our being? Why is it then that I don't experience these blessings all the time? I'm sorry to admit that I don't always feel the Spirit inside of me. I sometimes don't trust that these gifts are really available. I let my weak human nature take over and deny that God could possibly love me enough bless a poor soul like me with these wonderful gifts.

But this outpouring of the Spirit is a clear sign of how much God loves me and wants to share His gifts with me every day of my life.

Psalm 91:10–12

No evil shall befall you, no affliction come near your tent. For God commands the angels to guard you in all your ways. With their hands they shall support you lest you strike your foot against a stone.

Recall that during the first temptation of Christ, the devil used a portion of this scripture to lure Jesus into sin. Satan said, "Jump from this high tower. Because You are the Son of God, the angels will catch You lest You dash Your foot against a stone."

I like to imagine that this scripture is actually written about me. I visualize that God is telling me no evil will befall me and He will send angels to guard me. I firmly believe He has sent me a guardian angel all my own. While this is a traditional Catholic belief, it is commonly accepted that each human being has been assigned to a guardian angel that is always with us to look out for our welfare, spiritual and physical.

Does this sound to you like a magical tale similar to the Tooth Fairy, Easter Bunny, or Santa Claus? It is not hard for me to picture an angel sitting on my shoulder. Actually, I find this quite comforting. On the other hand, I can think of circumstances when my actions would have seriously embarrassed my angel—and me. I often pray for the Lord to help me to feel the presence of my guardian angel at all times. I thank Him for sending me this guide and helper, and ask that the angel will help me find my way along the path of life and protect me always.

Proverbs 18:22

He who finds a wife finds happiness; it is a favor he receives from the Lord.

I have the greatest respect for those who lead a single life, especially those who have made lifelong vows of celibacy and chastity in the priesthood, brotherhood, or as religious women.

For the men who have chosen married life, this verse resonates for a different reason. A loving, supportive wife is a tremendous blessing to any man. Like all lifelong commitments, marriages inevitably go through periods of strength and periods of weakness. It would be a rare marriage that went through neither. And more often than not, when the seas get rough, the gentle woman seems to be the one who calms them.

I offer the Lord my profound thanks for the wonderful woman He brought into my life to be my spouse, partner, and helpmate. My life has been greatly enriched by her love, counsel, and willingness to stand by me in times of distress. As the scripture says, the Lord has surely blessed me.

Matthew 5:1–12

The Sermon on the Mount: The Beatitudes
(For complete scripture text, see endnotes).

Jesus designates nine types of people for special blessings. Many fall into more than one category, I suppose. I wonder if I belong to some, or all, of these groups? Even after a lot of reading, I'm not completely sure what some of the designations mean.

Does "poor in spirit" mean you're detached from the world? I would probably get a "C" grade on that one.

Do "those who mourn" also include those who grieve for the declining moral standards of our society?

Who are "the meek?" Are they shy, self-effacing individuals who cannot promote themselves? Or are they the ones who understand that every gift they possess is a gift from God to be used for His glory?

What about he who "hungers and thirsts for righteousness?" Certainly, it doesn't mean those who are self-righteous.

The "merciful" are easy to spot because they are, unfortunately, small in number. I am among the many who are usually not inclined to extend mercy, forgiveness, and reconciliation to those who have offended us.

The "clean of heart" try to cooperate with God's graces to live a moral, productive, pious life. I get another "C" for that one.

And, ah, "the peacemakers." It is easy to understand why God would bless them. There is so much peace that is yet to be brokered in our homes, communities, nations, and the world. Anyone who carries out this task is entitled to be called a "child of God."

Those "persecuted for the sake of righteousness" must be those who have stood up to defend their beliefs and principles against withering, unjust attacks. Peter, Paul, Stephen—and Jesus—come to mind.

Finally, those who are "insulted and persecuted" because of Jesus will receive a reward great in heaven.

Like many scripture passages, these are lofty goals. The Beatitudes represent a powerful list of values that I should strive to include in daily life. Unfortunately, my weak human spirit fails to execute the plan God has laid out before me. Blessed be those, I say to the Lord, who want to do Your will. We need enormous help and many graces from Him to accomplish this.

Matthew 10:19–20

When they hand you over, do not worry about how you are to speak or what you are to say. You will be given at that moment what you are to say. For it will not be you who speaks but the Spirit of your Father speaking through you.

I have taken comfort from these words many times. My hands are a little clammy and my throat dry as I stand in front of a parish council, a group of people inquiring about my faith, or at the podium on Sunday begging for funds to help a sister parish in Honduras. Yes, I prepared in advance—but I know the "right" words that I speak will not be mine, but the Spirit's.

These kinds of situations represent excellent opportunities to turn things over to God. I have shared this passage with others who were nervously awaiting their turn to speak on some important matter. They, too, felt a calmness settle over them as they remember God's promise.

How can we fail when the Spirit is in our corner? Let us thank the Lord for sending these special graces when they are most needed.

Matthew 16:18–19

And so I say to you, you are Peter, and upon this rock I will build my church, and the gates of the netherworld shall not prevail against it. I will give you the keys to the kingdom of heaven. Whatever you bind on earth shall be bound in heaven; and whatever you loose on earth will be loosed in heaven.

This impetuous, simple fisherman lacked formal education. He was the rawest of men, this Simon. Yet, Jesus picked him to be the first leader of this new religion and to be the foundation of the church. In a whimsical, but meaningful, play on words, Jesus changed Simon's name to Peter (which, in Aramaic, means "Rock") as He commissioned him to accept this awesome charge.

Jesus also made a profound promise that no evil, human or supernatural, would take down His church till the end of all time.

This scripture says three important things to me. First, God always seems to choose ordinary people to achieve extraordinary things. Rock, or Peter, could hardly have been less distinguished, talented, or inspired. He wasn't even very faithful, having denied Jesus publicly three times the night before Jesus' agony and death. Yet, Peter was Jesus' clear choice for an overwhelming assignment.

We see exactly the same thing happen over and over again in our own lifetime. Mother Teresa of Calcutta, Pope John XXIII, and Martin Luther King, Jr. are clear examples of simple, unpretentious people chosen by God to effect enormous good in our world. Any of us selected by God for important work in building up His kingdom need only cooperate with the graces we will be given to get the job done.

We must remember, too, that the handful of apostles and disciples that Peter led were full of doubts, weaknesses, and misguided purposes. As years and centuries passed, those called Christians often fought with each other, created schisms, committed heresy, and fragmented into various sects, all of which battered the church. Even many church leaders turned out to be corrupt, greedy, and licentious. Is there a more perfect formula for collapse? Yet Jesus' promise endures.

The church founded by Jesus continues to grow and promote His teachings to every corner of the earth. Is the human church perfect? No, but thanks to God's promise, it is yet strong.

Finally, God trusted His weak human creatures to choose correctly when difficult decisions and judgments had to be made. I thank the Holy Spirit for being faithful to the fragile and finite humans who work to continue Jesus' mission on earth even to this present age. We humbly acknowledge that this could not have been achieved without You.

Luke 17:17–18

Ten (lepers) were cleansed, were they not? Where are the other nine? Has none but this foreigner returned to give thanks to God?

Oh, how we pray for God's help when we are facing some crisis or tragedy in our life. "Help me, Lord," I bellow, "save me from this terrible event that is about to overcome me and my loved ones!" And what happens then? My gracious Lord answers my prayer and removes me from harm's way.

Just like the ten lepers who were cured and returned into their community, I too have been saved from some perceived disaster. What is my response to God's fortuitous intervention? Do I immediately drop to my knees and thank Him profusely for His gifts?

The story about the ten lepers is instructive. Jesus cured all ten, but only one returned to thank Him. And the one who came back was a hated foreigner, a Samaritan. It has been said that if we could offer only one prayer, it should be one of thanksgiving. I need the Lord's help and reminder that He is so generous to me every moment of my life. I thank Him now for past gifts, for present graces, and for future blessings.

1 Chronicles 16:34

Give thanks to the Lord, for He is good, for His kindness endures forever.

>This simple verse is also a profound prayer. I give thanks to the Lord because He is so good to me. Regardless my frequent unfaithfulness, truly God's kindness to me endures forever.
>
>The Father is consistently kind to me. A simple "thank you" is so inadequate. I am compelled to drop to my knees and with bowed head to offer my sincere thanks for His blessings.

1 Corinthians 15:22–23

For just as in Adam all die; so too in Christ shall all be brought to life, but to each one in proper order; Christ the first fruits; then at his coming, those who belong to Christ.

>All humans paid a price for Adam's original sin. By the sweat of our brows we must earn our daily bread and, at last, all shall die. But we are not left hopeless. The Father promised to send His Son to be our Savior and to re-open the gates of heaven.
>
>And so He did! To fulfill God's covenant, Jesus was incarnated in human form, lived, suffered, died, was resurrected, and returned to sit at the Father's right hand.
>
>First, Jesus returned to His celestial home. Following that, all of us who belong to Jesus can expect the same happy fate. I am so grateful for Jesus' obedience to the Father and His willingness to prepare a heavenly home for me. Nothing I have done could earn such a gift. Only His all-embracing love for me has made this possible. I am full of nothing but gratitude for the Gracious God's unspeakable love and mercy toward me.

Colossians 3:17

And whatever you do, in word or in deed, do everything in the name of the Lord Jesus, giving thanks to God the Father through him.

When I was a freshman in college, one of my instructors, a Jesuit priest, always put the initials "AMDG" at the top center of the blackboard just before class began. I asked others what it meant, but heard only guesses or hunches.

Finally, after one class I got up the courage to ask the priest about the letters. He told me they stood for *ad majorem dei gloriam*, which when translated into English means "everything to the glory of God." He patiently explained to me that whatever we do, we should try to do it for God's glory.

Teaching, studying, playing sports, working at a job, being at leisure—everything we do can be offered up to the glory of God. That concept learned many years ago has stuck with me throughout my life. I often forget it, but I try to complete my activities for the splendor of the Lord's Almighty existence among us. For me, this represents an important way that I can offer my thanks for all the Lord has given to me.

I pray that the Lord helps me remember *ad majorem dei gloriam* more often, so that what I do in life reflects His glory and acts as a prayer of thanks.

1 Thessalonians 5:16–18

Rejoice always. Pray without ceasing. In all circumstances give thanks, for this is the will of God for you in Christ Jesus.

As a little boy I was taught to pray first thing in the morning in a special way. I was to say, "Lord, I offer to You everything I do this day. If somehow I forget about You during the day, please don't forget about me." In other words, I was instructed to pray without ceasing—even during the times I was too busy or forgot.

Later in life, I was told that if I could say but one prayer each day, it should be a prayer of thanksgiving for all God had done for me.

Whether young or old, this passage offers good advice. First, rejoice always. I am called to do my best to be full of the Lord's joy and happiness. Second, never stop praying. It doesn't mean that I must walk around with my hands folded and my eyes lifted to the skies. It does mean that I must try to keep God in the foreground of my consciousness, not the background.

Finally, the passage reminds me to give thanks to God in all situations. What wonderful counsel this is! I may sometimes forget or be distracted, so I pray to the Lord to provide transforming graces—and to remind me to rejoice always, pray without ceasing, and give thanks to Him every waking moment of my life.

Revelation 1:19

Write down, therefore, what you have seen, and what is happening, and what will happen afterwards.

That's what this book is about—telling what I've seen and experienced, how I feel about that, and what I perceive is happening around me. What will happen afterwards is anyone's guess, and I certainly don't have a crystal ball. I have taken on this book project—like my three previous books—because I felt a need to share my ideas with others.

I believe I have a good understanding of my writing ability. No matter how much I read others' work or practice the craft myself, I will never be a great writer. Adequate, maybe. Good, perhaps. But never great. But I also know that there are anonymous people out there who will read my work and be touched in some way because of

God's abundant grace. I would have expended the effort to complete this book if I thought only one person would benefit.

I thank God for the writing talent He has loaned me, the fortitude to finish this work, and the means to distribute it to others. I pray to Him that some who pick up this book be affected positively by what they read. May He grace them with a special insight, a sense of longing, or a gentle touch that leads them to Him more fully.

Matthew 24:35–36, 44

Heaven and earth will pass away, but my words will not pass away. But of that day and hour no one knows, neither the angels of heaven nor the Son, but the Father alone. So, too, you must be prepared, for at an hour you do not expect, the Son of Man will come.

I clearly remember when I was a young man. I was sure I was bulletproof. I engaged in some activities that would have turned my mother's hair white had she known. Probably the worst thing I did was riding a motor scooter to and from my army duty over highways and busy streets—with a cotton garrison cap as my only protection. Never mind; I was young, tough, and not subject to the laws of physics.

Much older now, much more creaky, and more clearly aware of how fragile my life is, I have a different mindset. Still, I find this passage sobering. I am going to pass from this life to the next *at an hour I do not expect.*

Oh, I know I will die some day. But there is still that small sense of denial that it could happen in the blink of an eye, even, perhaps, while I am typing these words. A massive heart attack or stroke, a burst artery, a freak accident or fall. One moment I am OK; the next I am face-to-face with my Creator.

I can think of too many situations where God's sudden appearance might have left me begging for His mercy. I believe one of God's great blessings to me is that I don't know what the future holds, and I must take God at His word: I must be ready always.

I ask that He help me keep the final prize always in my sight, and give me the grace of a happy death.

Mark 9:37

Whoever receives one child such as this in my name, receives me; and whoever receives me, receives not me but the one who sent me.

I have been greatly blessed in fathering six children. My children have given me fourteen grandchildren. When the children were little, I often thought they would never grow up. Sometimes the burden of caring and providing for them was overwhelming for my wife and me. While I think we did our best to give our children love, security, discipline, a sense of responsibility, and independence, I am sure we failed many times—especially me.

This scripture speaks to me about children's beautiful innocence and trust. A child allows the father to hold him and has no fear of being dropped. A child trusts parents to heal a minor scrape, wipe away a tear, or comfort some form of distress. When we treat the child with gentleness and love, it is a way to accept Jesus into our life.

Do I welcome Jesus into my heart with hug and little kiss? Do I have complete trust in the Lord that He will provide for me? Do I always recognize the unconditional love Jesus expresses for me? Do I understand that the way I receive a child is like the way I receive Jesus and God the Father?

I pray that the Lord will help me receive Him and the Father with childlike faith and love. Too often I lose sight of this lovely metaphor.

Luke 21:1–4

When he looked up he saw some wealthy people putting their offerings into the treasury and he noticed a poor widow putting in two small coins. He said, "I tell you truly, this poor widow put in more than all the rest; for those others have all made offerings from their surplus wealth, but she, from her poverty, has offered her whole livelihood."

Here is another dilemma for the Christian soul. What does it mean to be generous? How much should I give to others who need my assistance?

It is said that we cannot be too generous with God. Measuring my generosity can never be done in absolute amounts of my personal wealth, available time or talents gifted to me by God. The key question, the one that must be answered to the satisfaction of my Lord and myself, is this: "Am I giving out of my *need* or out of my *plenty?*"

From personal experience as a fund raiser for a new parish church, I can tell you how difficult it is for people to give generously. I saw single mothers dig very deep from their need to make a pledge to the new church. I also saw too many people who created elaborate excuses for why they could not make a substantial gift (God, forgive my judgmentalism). Giving from one's need means the gift hurts, at least a little. No matter how large the absolute gift, an offering from "what is left over" is never enough and unworthy.

Do I trust the Lord enough to give from my need? It means I must sacrifice something I had planned on acquiring or doing. How hard it is to handle my resources in a truly generous way. I pray that the Lord will help me overcome my greed and fear about how much money I have.

1 Corinthians 12:4–6

There are different kinds of spiritual gifts but the same Spirit; there are different forms of service but the same Lord; there are different workings but the same God who produces all of them in everyone.

We are a diverse lot. God has made each of us unique and granted us different gifts. The message I get from these verses is that God is unchanging and immutable, but we humans are all over the map with our skills and the types of service we perform.

Just look at a typical parish church community. People step forward to perform all manner of functions like ushering, cleaning the church building, folding the weekly bulletin, cooking at the pancake breakfast, or helping out with landscaping and maintenance. Some of those jobs don't require a lot of skill, just a cheerful willingness to do them. We also find talented musicians to lead the singing, teachers for the pre-school classes, those to proclaim the liturgical readings at Mass, technical experts to keep the church computer network maintained, and leaders for adult education classes.

Many of these people are talented and have highly developed skills. Different gifts and different service—does God really ascribe different values to these individuals? I don't think so. All of them are pulling on the oars, keeping the parish boat going forward.

May the Lord let me see the strength in the diversity of the people who are building His kingdom here on earth. May he show me how I fit into this mosaic and help me step forward to do what I have been gifted to do—nothing more and nothing less.

Galatians 3:28

There is neither Jew nor Greek, there is neither slave nor free person, there is not male and female; for you are all one in Christ Jesus.

I suppose it is human nature to want membership in exclusive clubs and organizations. It's comfortable to associate with those we consider to be "like us" in many ways. If we had a choice, we might even be willing to exclude certain people or groups from associations we belong to. I mean, you wouldn't ask me to be seen with people of the wrong political party, without a degree from an "important" college, or without the appropriate family pedigree—would you?

"Oh, yes, I would," says the Lord. "I came to save *all* people: Jews, Muslims, Catholics, Protestants; rich and poor; black, yellow, brown and white; male and female; haughty and humble; liberal and conservative." We are all members of the Body of Christ. If there is sickness in one part of the body, all of us hurt.

No matter how hard it may be for me, I pray that the Lord lets me see everyone as my brother or sister. He loves me—and all others—unconditionally and equally. Every time I start to feel superior to someone else, may He help me to remember that all of us share this gift of His almighty love.

Proverbs 17:6

Grandchildren are the crown of old men, and the glory of children is their parentage.

This verse is abundantly true in my own life. I have been blessed to have fourteen grandchildren—nine girls and five boys. Like my own children, each grandkid is unique and possesses a diverse personality.

Due to geographical separation, I see some of them infrequently. I find that each one is more or less loving, gregarious, animated, open with me, or shy. I confess to loving each of them deeply but (this is human nature) I like some more than others. But, there is plenty of love to spread around and I thoroughly enjoy my interaction with each and every one.

I thank the Father for permitting me to be a grandfather. I am so proud of these kids. I pray that He cares for them, because I won't be around forever, and may He touch them when the time is appropriate. May He show them His face and His love, and bless them with His saving graces.

1 John 2:15

Do not love the world or the things of the world. If anyone loves the world, the love of the Father is not in him.

There are so many wonderful people, places, and things on our planet. I think of my family as terrific, our extended family as—well, maybe not terrific always, but quirky and lovable, and my friends like precious gems. I am enthralled with the spectacular places on earth, such as Ireland, Australia, Germany, Switzerland, Italy, New Zealand, Mexico and Canada, and of course the United States of America.

I thoroughly enjoy good food and drink, pleasant surroundings, leisurely vacations, and the "good life" in general. Am I, and people who share my tastes, the objects of this scripture verse? Are we empty shells seeking good times but possessing no indwelling of the Father? Maybe—but maybe not.

I do not think God wants us to lead unhappy lives. He has put splendorous things before us to enjoy. For me, the problem comes when these transient, human delights become more important than my love of God and neighbor. Or when my pursuit of *la dolce vita* conflicts with my need to share my belongings with the poor.

I pray for the ability to see a clear distinction between keeping the Lord as the main focus of my life and seeking pleasurable things for their own sake. I want both His indwelling and the opportunity to enjoy His creation. May he always help me maintain the correct balance each day of my life.

Luke 12:48

Much will be required of the person entrusted with much, and still more will be demanded of the person entrusted with more.

I'll be honest. I don't like this passage. God has abundantly blessed me with gifts, and frankly, I'm good at doing a lot of human things. I also have a well-developed sense of these strengths, and of where my fragile human spirit fails.

This passage is very much a "good news–bad news" proposition. Because God has entrusted me with numerous gifts, He tells me that a lot more will be expected from me than from those not so gifted. Not fair! Why is more demanded of me? I want to say, "God, please tell others to carry a share of the load, too."

God answers no. He says, "I have entrusted these gifts to you so that you can use them to build my kingdom where I place you. I have other things planned for those who have received lesser gifts. It's none of your business what they do; you focus on what I want *you* to do."

I would like to argue with Him about this, but I know He is right. I pray that He gives me the grace to use my gifts well.

SUPPLICATION

Matthew 7:21

Not everyone who says to me, "Lord, Lord," will enter the kingdom of heaven, but only the one who does the will of my Father in heaven.

It's said that there are no atheists in foxholes. We also are told there will always be prayer in public schools as long as there are final exams. Stories about people bargaining with God are many: "If you will only give me this important thing I want or need, I will do the following for You, My Lord."

Sometimes I call out the Lord's name very loudly just hoping that my voice will rise above the din of millions of other prayers. But He tells me it doesn't help much just to announce His name. Those who enter the kingdom of heaven will be the ones who have done His will.

Like others, I am guilty of compartmentalizing my religious experience. Yes, there is always time for an hour or two at church each week, attending the liturgies. But, goes the reasoning, for the other 166 hours, please don't bother me because I have many human cares to deal with.

Mistake, says God. He knows I am human and weak, but wants me to live my life doing my best to enact his will. To that, I say, "OK, Lord, I'll try. But please understand I will probably fail often."

Matthew 16:24–26

Whoever wishes to come after me must deny himself, take up his cross and follow me. For whoever wishes to save his life will lose it, but whoever loses his life for my sake will find it. What profit would there be for one to gain the whole world and forfeit his life? Or what can one give in exchange for his life?

There is a haunting and somewhat uneasy message for me in these three verses from Matthew. First, I am told to deny myself. Deny myself what? Earthly comforts? A materialistic lifestyle? Selfish ambition?

Then I am told to take up my cross. I don't know a single person who does not have a cross of some kind to bear. Is it poor health? Broken relationships with family? Lack of financial security? Limited opportunity because of poor education? Jesus tells me to pick my personal cross (without grumbling, I think) and follow Him just as He did on that fateful Friday heading to Calvary. I have often said to Him, "I will dutifully pick up my cross as you ask—just don't make it too heavy."

And what is the meaning of "saving" and "losing" life for His sake? Is Jesus really talking about life and death? Or does He mean that His followers must reject attachment to the things of this world?

And then, the final, grand instruction. If I turn out to be the richest, most famous and popular person on earth, what good is that if it causes me to lose eternal life with God? The venal, hedonistic and self-indulgent life may be alluring, but I must focus on my daily fidelity, and show daily love toward God and my neighbor.

I pray to the Lord to each day help me focus on an eternal life lived in His presence.

Matthew 21:22

Whatever you ask for in prayer with faith, you will receive.

It seems to me the operative words in this verse from Matthew are *with faith*. I petition God all the time, listing my needs in great detail. "Please give me this, Lord, and that, too, and a whole list of other things I think I want…" Of course, He already knows what I need long before I form my prayer, but He listens patiently.

I'm sorry to say that a lot of time I do not offer these petitions *with faith*. I am guilty of filling God's ears with my prayers, while not seriously expecting that they will be fulfilled. *With faith* does implies not only an expectation that my prayers might be answered; it also means that I accept God's divine wisdom that determines which of my prayers are sincere, which are good for me, and which will glorify Him.

I sincerely believe that all my prayers are answered. It's just that the answer may not be the one I expected and may be a surprise to me. I will pray, then, for the Lord's help in offering all my prayers to Him *with faith*.

Mark 6:50b

"Take courage, it is I, do not be afraid."

The great Pope John Paul II often used the phrase, "Do not be afraid." His message was that God the Father, Son, and Holy Spirit were always there to prop us up when our human frailty left us fearful and trembling.

This verse comes from the apostles' account of Jesus walking on the water toward their boat. Like any human being, these men were terrified. In my own life, I see many things that strike terror in my heart—a child's failed marriage, the threat of a serious illness a family member, or a loved one's misguided decision which will adversely affect their future.

My flawed first reaction is to try and regain control of the situation. Why do I always think I can be in control? What I should be doing is turning to God for help. He gently says to me, "Have courage; I am your God; do not be afraid of this situation. I will assist you." I am so thankful for His boundless love and mercy towards me, and for his constant presence at my side.

Exodus 3:11

But Moses said to God, "Who am I that I should go to Pharaoh and lead the Israelites out of Egypt?"

I can just picture Moses speaking to God: "You want ME to do WHAT? I have absolutely no skill or talent that qualifies me for this job. Go pick on someone else and please leave me alone." Moses, the stutterer, wanted no part of this task the Lord called him to do.

How often each of us behaves like Moses! We are called upon to head up a church committee, create some type of new program to assist the poor, or organize a fundraiser. "Not me," we cry. "I don't have the time or talent for such a job. Besides, there are others who are much more qualified. Call on them!"

God expects a different response. He is counting on us to accept the fact that He has blessed us with unique gifts. He wants us to use these gifts in ways that give Him honor and glory. He also wants us to stretch, to get out of our comfort zone. In short, God is looking for us to build up the kingdom where we live, work and play.

I pray that the Lord gives me the courage to say yes when called to do His labor here on earth. I find it much easier to avoid these tasks, but with His help I may be able to step up and accept my responsibilities.

Luke 12:22–24

Therefore I tell you, do not worry about your life and what you will eat, or about your body and what you will wear. For life is more than clothing. Notice the ravens: they do not sow or reap; they have neither storehouse nor barn, yet God feeds them. How much more important are you than birds!

>This is easy to understand, but hard to live out in real life. Who among us has not worried about material safety? I certainly have, perhaps inordinately so. Now in the twilight of my life, I wonder if my savings will see my wife and me through to the end. How I would hate to call upon my children to contribute to our keep! They have their own financial struggles, saving for college educations and their own retirement.
>
>Jesus' example is so apt. During the spring and summer, we can observe the tiny goldfinches flitting from flower to bush to tree in the garden outside our windows. They are beautiful little creatures. They have no worries—well, except for the fat squirrel that stalks but never catches them.
>
>I am guilty of wanting to be in control, making sure I have enough. Trust in God is so hard for me. I know I experience divine, unconditional love. Why, then, am I afraid to turn things over to God? I am weak, so I need His grace.

Luke 12:34

For where your treasure is, there also will your heart be.

>I don't think *treasure* refers only to money in this verse. Anything that becomes unduly important to me can become my treasure and thus can control my heart.
>
>Consider the effect of a consuming desire for success in business, a concentrated focus on hedonistic pleasure, or seeking personal or political power at any cost. Could

these, and similar things, become my treasure in this life? If they did, they probably would control my heart as well.

Once again, I must turn to the Lord for help. There is a lure in all these "treasures" that can lead my spiritual life astray. Jesus helps me understand that the real treasure in this life and the next consists of leading a Christian life.

1 Corinthians 9:24

Do you not know that the runners in the stadium all run in the race, but only one wins the prize? Run so as to win.

We have all seen thrilling television coverage from the Olympic Games. The marathon is especially exciting. The packed stadium hums in expectation, awaiting the entrance of the runners through a tunnel. Although the race is over 26 miles long, there are often several participants neck-and-neck entering the stadium for the final 440 yards. Even those miles have not permitted the athletes to separate themselves from the other able runners. They have struggled for well over two hours, and now it comes down to just a few feet separating the best of the best. Finally, only one can win; no one remembers the name of the second-place finisher.

The writer of this passage uses the analogy to instruct us about our lives. Birth to death can be compared to a long race. We are urged to run this marathon toward eternal life with everything we have. Eternal life is our prize, so we are advised to run for victory. Lord knows, sometimes life leaves me breathless and exhausted. I don't think I can carry on without His help. I pray to Jesus to show me how to pace myself and endure the long and difficult contest. I want to win the race and live my eternal life in His presence.

1 Corinthians 13:1, 13

If I speak in human and angelic tongues but do not have love, I am a resounding gong or a clashing cymbal. So faith, hope and love remain, these three; but the greatest of these is love.

> This passage can be unsettling for me. It refers to three mighty virtues: faith, hope and love. Do I have faith? I believe I do. While I cannot see God with my human eyes, I firmly believe in a Triune God. I believe that Jesus took the form of a man, died and rose from the dead to open the gates of heaven for all people.
>
> What about hope? I know that God is all-loving and all-merciful, and I am inspired by His promise of an eternity of bliss for those who believe and keep His word.
>
> But love—I am not so sure about that. Love is called the greatest of these virtues, and it is where I often fail. My love for God seems too often to be distracted and lukewarm. My love for my family is too often conditional. My love for friends often depends on the circumstance. My love for mankind is frequently withheld, and denied to those whom I sense are enemies. How do I overcome my human weakness and fully develop the virtue of love? I don't know how to do this, and must ask the Lord for continued aid.

1 Corinthians 16:13

Be on your guard, stand firm in the faith, be courageous, be strong.

> We are taught from youth that one of the gifts of the Holy Spirit is fortitude. This verse warns us how important it is to be alert and persistent in our faith.
>
> It is easy to drift along from day to day, believing we are living a good, pious life, and following the path to eternal life with God. Spiritual complacence is an insidious trap. When we least expect it, some event can rock our life

and cause us to question our faith. This can happen to anyone—even me, even you. Therefore, we are advised not only to turn to God daily for whatever sustenance we need, but to be courageous in our vigilance.

This short verse calls us to four separate actions: vigilance, firmness, courage, and strength. As with all other things, we cannot do this without God's graces. We can pray to be given what we need to do all the things He asks of us on a daily basis.

Philippians 4:6–7

Have no anxiety at all, but in everything, by prayer and petition, with thanksgiving, make your requests known to God. Then the peace of God that surpasses all understanding will guard your hearts and minds in Christ Jesus.

Anxiety is a constant companion in many people's lives. Parents worry about maintaining a reliable stream of income to satisfy all the financial obligations of a family. Children worry about how they are doing in school and agonize about getting good grades so they can be accepted to prestigious universities. Grandparents worry about both their children and grandchildren and the changing world that they must face in the future. Singles worry about meeting and attracting a suitable mate with whom to spend their lives. Seniors worry about the onset of debilitating illness that can make old age a tortuous and pain-filled experience.

With all this apprehension, peace is not a common experience for many folks. The Lord tells me that I can gain a sense of peace if I follow the formula He provides. Prayers of thanksgiving and petition are a good way to begin. I must tell God what I need and confidently expect He will grant my requests if it is His will. Most importantly, I should request this peace that my heart craves. I believe that the Lord will send this peace "which surpasses all understanding" to guard my heart. I accept this as true, and I turn to Him to make it happen.

2 Timothy 1:7

For God did not give us a spirit of cowardice but rather of power and love and self-control.

How many times in your spiritual or religious life have you felt a sense of cowardice? Ever found yourself faced with a scripture-quoting zealot spewing hatred for your church in the name of God? Nervously laughing at crude or racially insulting jokes so you wouldn't stand out in the crowd? Failing to stand up and do the right thing because it would have been awkward?

We have all had these moments that called for bravery but unmasked us as cowards. That is not the spirit God wants for us. He has provided us His graces and unconditional love so that we can exercise power, love, and self-control even in the most difficult or unnerving situations. As William Shakespeare wrote, "Cowards die many times before their deaths; the valiant never taste of death but once."

I ask the Father to give me the courage and power to act valiantly, especially when I face difficult circumstances. I wish to stand up for my faith, my beliefs and my God when I, or they, are attacked by seemingly overwhelming powers.

Hebrews 13:6

Thus we say with confidence: The Lord is my helper, I will not be afraid. What can anyone do to me?

Almost everyone has faced disquieting and scary moments in life. Maybe you've had a physical encounter with an aggressive person. Perhaps there was a serious automobile accident, or your house has been burgled. A medical professional may have told you that you face a life-threatening illness.

A multitude of situations get our hearts pumping, the adrenalin flowing, and raise a lump of fear in our parched throats. In almost every case we feel alone in our distress.

In those times I must ask myself—do I really believe that the Lord is standing beside me, ready to act as my helper? My faith tells me that I am unconditionally loved by God, who always wants to protect me. Still, it isn't easy to have total trust in God's presence and His willingness to help.

I pray to Gentle Jesus that when I face these difficult moments in my life, I am given the grace of belief and reliance on Him. For when I sense Him at my side, I am sure no one can do anything to harm me. May He instill in me the comfort, trust, and peace that I need to turn to Him in times of personal trouble or spiritual peril.

3 John 1:4

Nothing gives me greater joy than to hear that my children are walking in the truth.

My wife and I raised our six children in a loving, observant Catholic home. All of the children had the benefit of a Catholic grammar school education; the three boys also attended a high school conducted by the Servite Fathers. No parents are perfect, but we did our best to share our faith with the kids in word and deed, and by example.

Now they are in their 40s and 50s. All seem to work hard at being good spouses, parents, and citizens. They appear to live moral, upstanding lives. Three of the kids attend a Catholic church. A couple of them attend evangelical churches more or less regularly. One does not attend church at all.

Would I be happier if all continued with their Catholic heritage? Of course, but it does not bother me that some of them may still be searching. I have full confidence that the Spirit will touch the heart of each child when the time is right. How will the kids respond? I don't know, but I believe in my core that none of my children has turned his or her back to God.

We parents have turned over our children to the Lord to care for. Let us pray that He give them all the love, mercy, and graces He has given us.

Isaiah 55:8–9

For My thoughts are not your thoughts, nor are your ways My ways, says the Lord. As high as the heavens are above the earth, so high are My ways above your ways and My thoughts above your thoughts.

I must remind myself that the clouded, finite intellect I inherited from Adam is not capable of understanding God's ways. When something happens that distresses me, I catch myself saying, "Why did God let that happen? What possible good can come out of that?" I become frustrated with the Lord because I do not understand what has taken place.

These words from Isaiah quickly bring me back to earth. The Lord's plan is infinite; my thought process is finite. I must, in faith, accept that God's ways are so great compared to my puny mind that I can never hope to fully understand what's going on. Instead of being angry or bitter at Isaiah's words, I feel a great sense of hope and calmness come over me. God, in His infinite wisdom and love, has established a plan for everyone and everything in the world.

Faith and trust are essential. I pray to the Lord Jesus to help me humbly accept that He is guiding the world with His almighty mind, and to give me a sense of peace.

Matthew 7:7–8

Ask and it will be given to you; seek and you will find; knock and the door will be opened to you. For everyone who asks, receives; and the one who seeks, finds; and to the one who knocks, the door will be opened.

Well, that sounds pretty easy. All I have to do is ask or seek or knock and everything I want or need will come true. That includes miracle cures for terminally ill loved ones, financial windfalls to solve impossible money difficulties, and complete reconciliation of horrendously broken relationships. If things don't turn out as I asked, at least I have someone to blame—God.

Yet I don't really think God wanted me to interpret this passage as a blank check. I believe I am instructed to turn to the Lord with all my needs, big and small. In His infinite love, He knows exactly what I need long before I even ask. The solutions that seem right to my cloudy, human, finite intellect may not always be part of God's plan for me. In my personal experience, He often answers my prayers of petition in His own way—and not the way I would have planned. Sometimes He answers no.

But God *does* want me to turn to Him in time of need. He also wants me to trust that He will give me what I need to get through any circumstance of life. So, we return to the issue of trust in God. To me, this is one of the most difficult things to do in my human life, one I struggle with everyday.

Matthew 23:12 and Luke 13:30

Whoever exalts himself will be humbled; but whoever humbles himself will be exalted.

For behold, some are last who will be first, and some are last who will be first.

I hear a stern warning in these two verses. God says I might *think* I am better than others, or *think* I deserve recognition. He tells me that this is disordered thinking. If I attempt to exalt myself, I will be quickly knocked down a peg. If I declare myself to be first, someone much better than I will quickly put me in my place at the back of the line.

Why does this happen? First, I am prone to cloudy, human thinking: I may have a totally misguided view of my own worth. Second, God demands humility, not pride, from his children. He tells me I can never be wrong to take the last place and to practice sincere humility.

My prayer, then, is that if I do climb up on my high horse and start to believe I am better than my neighbor, the Lord will knock me down just as he chastised Saul. It is easy for me to be proud, and I need the Lord's graces to know and keep my place.

Mark 7:21–23

From within people, from their hearts, come evil thoughts, unchastity, theft, murder, adultery, greed, malice, deceit, licentiousness, envy, blasphemy, arrogance, folly. All these evils come from within and they defile.

It is easy to blame others for my own sins, faults and failings. I can convince myself that I would never have done this or that dreadful thing except for the negative influence of some person or some thing. Hey, it's not my fault! Anybody can see that—can't they?

But Jesus says my argument is invalid. When I turn my back on God and tell Him to get out of my life—my definition of sin—it is I who have failed to cooperate with God's grace. This scripture is about my need to accept personal responsibility.

Sure, the devil is truly alive, roaming the earth looking for those he can seduce into sin. I have encountered him more times than I like to admit. Faced with the devil's blandishments, Judas chose one path; the good thief crucified with Jesus chose another. I have the same choice.

I must ask for the Lord's assistance when I am sorely tempted, and hope he will help me accept His outpouring of graces so that I can suppress these evils and keep myself undefiled.

Mark 10:51

Jesus said to him, "What do you want me to do for you?" The blind man replied to him, "Master, I want to see."

The blind man in Mark's story replied to Jesus' question with passion and pleading. He had probably spent his life sightless. He may also have heard about Jesus' reputation for healing people with various afflictions. Given the opportunity, he begged to be cured.

In the quiet of my prayer time, I can hear Jesus saying to me, "What do you want Me to do for you?" Although my eyesight has begun to wane, I have enjoyed good vision most of my life. And yet, my response to Jesus' question should be the same: "Master, that I may see!" See what? The pathway I am to walk to build God's kingdom; my neighbor's needs, so that I may help alleviate them; the role I can play as a peacemaker in my community; places where my love, compassion, and caring can make a difference; all the things I must do to achieve eternal life with God.

My Jesus let me see all these things—and more. I don't want to be blind to the people, places, and things which my actions could help, or to the opportunities to glorify His name.

1 Corinthians 10:13

No trial has come to you but what is human. God is faithful and will not let you be tried beyond your strength; but with the trial he will also provide a way out, that you may be able to bear it.

Looking back over my relatively long life, I have traveled mostly along a broad, gentle path with only a few potholes or rocky stretches. Compared to most, I have endured little suffering, pain, or heartache.

Humanly, this concerns me. I know that few of us are spared trials that severely test our spirit. As each new day dawns, I wonder when the other shoe is going to drop. Will I be able to maintain my faith, my hope, my optimism about the future? I am supposed to believe that I will not be tested beyond my strength. But, I must cooperate with God's graces to weather a storm. Do I have the spiritual reserves to cooperate with the type of help the Lord will offer? I must wait to find out. Meanwhile, I pray.

Galatians 6:9

Let us not grow tired of doing good, for in due time we shall reap our harvest, if we do not give up.

I go along day after day trying to do good things in my community and for my neighbors. Well, at least *most* of the time—or, at a minimum, *some* of the time. OK, OK, sometimes I neither try hard nor do good things.

Why do I occasionally grow tired of lending a hand, pitching in to help, volunteering for some task or just being an attentive friend? Maybe I feel used by someone who is taking advantage of me. Maybe I think I've been requested to do something that is just silly or unnecessary. Maybe my helping hand is criticized as insufficient by a grumpy recipient having an off-day. For whatever reason—perhaps just my own bad mood—I grow tired of doing good. "The heck with it," I sputter, "let somebody else do all the good work for awhile. I'm weary of always being the one to do it."

When that happens, the Lord says to me, "Come on, life is not as glum as you think. Keep plugging away, give yourself daily to the place where you live and work and to the people who share your community life. I promise you," He says, "if you hang in there and don't give up, I will make it worthwhile for you in the end."

I get the message, and I accept it, but sometimes it just isn't easy to follow His call. When I feel discouraged and want to quit, I must pray for the stamina and fortitude to continue building His kingdom in my community and with my neighbors.

Ephesians 6:13

Therefore, put on the armor of God that you may be able to resist on the evil day and have done everything to hold your ground.

Our modern day combat soldiers look something like the gladiators of old. Helmets, bullet resistant vests, and other protection are standard issue. Military leaders are doing everything possible to protect our young soldiers from the violence of enemy weaponry.

There is an analogy here to our existence. As we go through life daily, we encounter many enemies who would harm us. Materialism, greed, envy, personal conflicts, and a hundred other things assault us constantly. They can be relentless hazards to us as we try to love God and our neighbor as we have been instructed.

What are we to do? If we are to keep safe from the dangers lurking around us, we must put on God's armor. His protection for us is grace, mercy, and His unconditional love for every human being. Only with this armor can I be protected from the evil that wants to kill my soul.

I ask the Lord to please send me His security shield today and everyday, and to help me hold my ground against the evil one who seeks to devour me.

2 Timothy 3:12

In fact, all who want to live religiously in Christ Jesus will be persecuted.

If asked, most people would not admit to being persecuted for their religion. We are all fortunate to live in a country where there is general religious tolerance and where all can practice their religious beliefs without fear of persecution.

So, what am I to make of this scripture verse? Persecution can take many forms, some of them brutal and repressive. Think of the thousands of Iraqi Christians who have recently been martyred and others driven out of their homeland. Consider the genocide in Africa, which affecting many Christians. Even in this country, we have seen an entire church vilified for the actions of a few aberrant priests. I personally have been spit upon while holding an anti-abortion sign outside a political gathering. I have heard the Pope called the anti-Christ. I listened while a TV preacher described my church as the "great whore of Babylon." I routinely see prime time TV which mocks any one who does not accept homosexuality, abortion, gay marriage, or other "alternative lifestyles." Those who profess to hold traditional, moral values are dismissed as "right-wing loons."

Is this persecution? Yes, I think it is. I have not yet had to suffer physical pain for my beliefs. Could that happen in the future? I believe it might. Increasing polarization between those who promote secular humanism and those who hold Christian values is almost sure to happen. Here is the key question: where will I stand if, and when, I face physical harm on account of my religion? Will I remain tall and brave—or will I cave in to the culture?

I ask the Mighty God to spare me from physical, mental, or emotional persecution based on my love for Him. But if I must face such a grim day, I pray that He gives me the strength, courage, and will to always profess that He is my God, who protects the persecuted.

Mark 11:24

Therefore, I tell you, all that you ask for in prayer, believe that you will receive it and it shall be yours.

Frequently the Bible tells us that when we ask God to give us something, with a belief that our wish will be granted, that we shall receive it. There are two points about all these passages that I try to remember.

First, God wants me to feel free to ask for things I think will improve my life or the lives of loved ones. He repeatedly tells me this throughout the scriptures, so I should pay attention and take His advice. He assures me that my prayers are heard.

Second, He tells me my prayers will be answered. So, why is it that some of the things I pray for do not happen? God, in His infinite wisdom, determines that many of the things I pray for would not make the desired improvement. While I truly believe that God answers all my prayers, I also think that the answers often differ from my expectations.

Does this make me disillusioned or disheartened? No, of course not. God *does* answer all prayers, and He ensures that what He sends us fits His plan for our lives and the lives of others. How fortunate we are to have such a loving God, one who does not permit us to have things that are not in His infinite plan for our lives.

I praise and thank Him for His great love and compassion for a poor servant like me.

Romans 12:18

If possible, on your part, live at peace with all.

I'm pleased that the writer put the words *if possible* at the beginning of this verse. I am told to live at peace with all. The opposite of "peace" is "conflict." Wouldn't you think that I would act in my own self-interest and live at peace with my neighbors? But often I don't, and sometimes you don't, and all too often nations and regions don't, either.

What can possibly so alluring in conflict, even war? It is so much easier and pleasant to have peaceful relations with everyone we know. Somehow human jealousies, envy, disdain for others' ideas, perceived insults, or basic human prejudices intervene and cause these nasty conflicts to flare up. The modifying phrase *if possible* shows us the writer understood human nature even two thousand years ago.

Often I am not in a position to influence the conflicts between large groups or nations. But it is always possible for me to control my actions towards the people I interact with daily. Therefore I must take this responsibility seriously. For the *if possible* part, I will rely on God's grace to help me keep my envy, jealousy, and disdain in check.

I must pray for the Lord's assistance to live each day in peace with every person I meet. If we all do that, this peace may spread and eventually eliminate the wider conflicts that are so pervasive in our world.

1 Corinthians 3:16

Do you not know that you are the temple of God, and that the Spirit of God dwells in you?

I don't always feel like I am the temple of God. I eat too much and weigh more than I should. I exercise regularly but don't feel in especially good shape. At my age, joints ache, eyes don't see so well, my heart has some funny rhythms and lots of my systems aren't running very effectively. This is a temple that needs one of those home makeovers you see on TV, along with a thorough cleaning and a fresh coat of paint.

We must take seriously the fact that the Spirit dwells in us. This magnificent human body is a gift from God, who co-created us with our parents. We should not abuse this temple. I think we need to ask ourselves some fairly stern questions on a regular basis. Do I smoke? Is my consumption of alcohol moderate? Am I careless about what types of food I eat? Do I regularly see a doctor and dentist and follow their prescriptions? Do I exercise on a regular, consistent basis? Do I always use my seatbelt and drive within the road rules? Do I take part in activities that are unnecessarily dangerous?

None of us can live inside a protective bubble, but we should take reasonable measures to preserve and protect this temple gifted to us by God. I thank the Lord for sending His Spirit to dwell within me, and ask His help in taking care of this vessel so that it gives honor to the One who lives within.

Psalm 71:9

Do not cast me aside in my old age; as my strength fails, do not forsake me.

This verse is so appropriate for me and my neighbors in the retirement community where we live. Almost all my friends have upbeat and positive dispositions, and yet I know everyone has assorted aches, pains, and even chronic illnesses. It's virtually impossible not to get a little "down" occasionally. The same is true of our spiritual lives. Things can be downright difficult when we grow old and our strength ebbs.

This verse encourages me to turn to God in those periods when dark moods or even depression take over. I turn to Him, asking that He not cast me aside and do not forsake me in my old age. I am sure God loves me deeply and without condition at every stage of my life. It just seems that I may need some extra help and support in old age, and for Jesus' constant attention, I am grateful.

Ephesians 2:8

For by grace you have been saved through faith, and this not from you; it is the gift of God.

I cannot be reminded enough of my faith. It is a magnificent gift from God and I have done nothing to deserve it. And as with all gifts, it can be withdrawn.

It is imperative that I nourish God's gift to me. I must daily lift up my prayer of thanks for having been so greatly blessed, and this is my prayer: "Lord, please keep this flower of faith growing in my heart throughout my earthly life. When it is time to meet You face-to-face, I hope You will find a beautiful garden in my soul. Thank You for being so generous with me."

1 Timothy 5:17

Presbyters who preside well deserve double honor, especially those who toil in preaching and teaching.

I have been truly blessed in my life to know many outstanding priests. I don't remember my parish priests during my growing-up years except for the one who taught me the Latin responses that all altar boys had to memorize to serve at Mass.

I had many wonderful friendships among the Jesuit Fathers when I was a university student. Four parish priests are an important part of my memory: Fr. Emmett McCarthy of St. Angela Merici Parish in Brea, California;

Fr. John Kerns of St. Francis Parish in Sherwood, Oregon; Fr. Dick Rossman of Resurrection Parish in Tualatin, Oregon and the current chaplain where I now live, Fr. Dick Berg, CSC, Mary's Woods in Lake Oswego, Oregon.

As this verse says, all these priests well deserve double honor because they preach and teach. I thank God for sending these wonderful men into my life. They have provided me with the sacraments, Mass, consolation, instruction, and encouragement. Most important, they have all been friends. They are just men, but they are very special men, each of them.

Sirach (Ecclesiasticus) 3:12–14a

My son, take care of your father when he is old; grieve him not as long as he lives. Even if his mind fails, be considerate with him; revile him not in the fullness of your strength. For kindness to a father will not be forgotten.

I know the Book of Sirach (Ecclesiasticus) is not a part of the Protestant Canon of Old Testament Scripture. So, forgive me, my non-Catholic friends, for making this a part of my book. Sirach is important to Catholics, especially in liturgy, but in deference to you, I have only selected one passage from it.

I just couldn't pass up these verses. I want my children to read them. I am provided with few opportunities to send them on even minor guilt trips, so this could be my final chance. (What good Catholic father has not dispensed some guilt to his kids?) So, my children, this particular scripture is for each of you. *Son* is completely interchangeable with *daughter*, in case you girls believe your gender gets you off the hook.

Since I am quickly approaching the time when these verses will apply, I ask each of you to carefully review—if not memorize—these words and be prepared to act upon them as needed.

In seriousness, I do ask the Lord to abundantly bless my children and grandchildren. I pray that He sends to each of them the graces and assistance they need to have a relationship with their Creator and to lead moral and productive lives. I love all these people dearly, and pray that He loves them, too.

Isaiah 55:10–11

For just as from the heavens the rain and snow come down and do not return there till they have watered the earth, making it fertile and fruitful, giving seed to him who sows and bread to him who eats, so shall My word be that goes forth from my mouth; it shall not return to Me void, but shall do My will, achieving the end for which I sent it.

You have just about reached the end of this book. What an apt way to describe the holy words of sacred scripture: "Rain and snow watering the earth making it fertile and fruitful." The purpose of this book is to be a conduit for the Holy Spirit to touch hearts with the inspired words of sacred scripture.

I have read these words and listened to the messages they wrote on my soul. I have tried to share my feelings with you, dear reader, about the way I have been changed, touched, and directed by selected passages of scripture. My fondest wish is that you, too, have somehow been changed. We share this great oneness, you and I, in the Body of Christ. I promise to include you in my prayers for as long as I live. I feel greatly humbled to pray for people I may not know, or have never met but who have shared ideas and prayers with me. Thank you for reading my book. May God the Father, Son and Holy Spirit abundantly bless you forever. Amen.

2 Maccabees 15 (Epilogue):37 (parts)

I will bring my own story to an end. ... If it is well written and to the point, that is what I wanted; if it is poorly done and mediocre, that is the best I could do. ... A skillfully composed story delights the ears of those who read the work. Let this, then, be the end.

Do you think I could possibly find a better way to end this book? Imagine—a scripture verse to draw all this to a close. I thank the Lord for letting me complete this work. May it touch many hearts.

ENDNOTES

Page 16, Luke 24:13–35, The Road to Emmaus

Now that very day two of them were going to a village seven miles from Jerusalem called Emmaus, and they were conversing about all the things that had occurred. And it happened that while they were conversing and debating, Jesus himself drew near and walked with them, but their eyes were prevented from recognizing him. He asked them, "What are you discussing as you walk along?" They stopped, looking downcast. One of them, named Cleopas, said to him in reply, "Are you the only visitor to Jerusalem who does not know of the things that have taken place there in these days?" And he replied to them, "What sort of things?" They said to him, "The things that happened to Jesus the Nazarene, who was a prophet mighty in deed and word before God and all the people, how our chief priests and rulers both handed him over to a sentence of death and crucified him. But we were hoping that he would be the one to redeem Israel, and besides all this, it now the third day since this took place. Some women from our group, however, have astounded us: they were at the tomb early in the morning and did not find his body; they came back and reported that they had indeed seen a vision of angels who announced that he was alive. Then some of those with us went to the tomb and found things just as the women had described, but him they did not see." And he said to them, "Oh, how foolish you are! How slow of heart to believe all that the prophets spoke! Was it not necessary that the Messiah should suffer these things and enter into his glory?" Then beginning with Moses and all the prophets, he interpreted to them what referred to him in all the scriptures. As they approached the village to which they were going, he gave the impression that he was going on farther. But they urged him, "Stay with us, for it is nearly evening and the day is almost over." So he went in to stay with them. And it happened that, while he was with them at table, he took bread, said the blessing, broke it, and gave it to them. With that their eyes were opened and they recognized him, but he vanished from their sight. Then they said to each other, "Were not our hearts burning within us while he spoke to us on the way and opened the scriptures to us?" So they set out at once and returned to Jerusalem where they found gathered together the eleven and those with them who were saying, "The Lord has truly been raised and has appeared to Simon!" Then the two recounted what had taken place on the way and how he was made known to them in the breaking of the bread.

Page 24, Matthew 13:1–9, The Parable of the Sower

On that day, Jesus went out of the house and sat down by the sea. Such large crowds gathered around him that he got into a boat and sat down, and the whole crowd stood along the shore. And he spoke to them at length in parables, saying: "A sower sent out to sow. And as he sowed, some seed fell on the path, and birds came and ate it up. Some fell on rocky ground, where it had little soil. It sprang up at once because the soil was not deep, and when the sun rose it was scorched, and it withered for lack of roots. Some seed fell among thorns, and the thorns grew up and choked it. But some seed fell on rich soil, and produced fruit, a hundred or sixty or thirtyfold. Whoever has ears ought to hear.

Page 52, Matthew 25:31–46, The Judgment of the Nations

When the Son of Man comes in his glory, and all the angels with him, he will sit upon his glorious throne, and all the nations will be assembled before him. And he will separate them one from another, as a shepherd separates the sheep from the goats. He will place the sheep on his right and the goats on his left. Then the king will say to those on his right, "Come, you who are blessed by my Father. Inherit the kingdom prepared for you from the foundation of the world. For I was hungry and you gave me food, I was thirsty and you gave me drink, a stranger and you welcomed me, naked and you clothed me, ill and you cared for me, in prison and you visited me." Then the righteous will answer him and say, "Lord, when did we see you hungry and feed you, or thirsty and give you drink? When did we see you a stranger and welcome you, or naked and clothe you? When did we see you ill or in prison, and visit you?" And the king will say to them in reply, "Amen, I say to you, whatever you did for one of these least brothers of mine, you did for me." Then he will say to those on his left, "Depart from me, you accursed, into the eternal fire prepared for the devil and his angels. For I was hungry and you gave me no food, I was thirsty and you gave me no drink, a stranger and you gave me no welcome, naked and you gave me no clothing, ill and in prison, and you did not care for me." And they will answer and say, Lord, when did we see you hungry or thirsty or a stranger or naked or ill or in prison and not minister to your needs?" He will answer them, "Amen, I say to you, what you did not do for one of these least ones, you did not do for me." And these will go off to eternal punishment, but the righteous to eternal life.

Page 67, Luke 15:11–32. The Parable of the Prodigal Son

Then he said, "A man had two sons, and the younger son said to his father, "Father, give me the share of your estate that should come to me." So the father divided the property between them. After a few days, the younger son collected all his belongings and set of to a distant country where he squandered his inheritance on a life of dissipation. When he had freely spent everything, a severe famine struck that country, and he found himself in dire need. So he hired himself out to one of the local citizens who sent him to his farm to tend the swine. And he longed to eat his fill of the pods on which the swine fed, but nobody gave him any. Coming to his senses he thought, "How many of my father's hired workers have more than enough food to eat, but here am I, dying from hunger. I shall get up and go to my father and I shall say to him, "Father, I have sinned against heaven and against you. I no longer deserve to be called your son; treat me as you would treat one of your hired workers." So he got up and went back to his father. While he was still a long way off, his father caught sight of him, and was filled with compassion. He rant to his son, embraced him and kissed him. His son said to him, "Father, I have sinned against heaven and against you; I no longer deserve to be called your son. But his father ordered his servants, "Quickly bring the finest robe and put it on him; put a ring on his finger and sandals on his feet. Take the fattened calf and slaughter it. Then let us celebrate with a feast, because this son of mine was dead, and has come to life; he was lost, and has been found." Then the celebration began. Now the older son had been out in the field and, on his way back, as he neared the house, he heard the sound of music and dancing. He called one of the servants and asked what this might mean. The servant said to him, "Your brother has returned and your father has slaughtered the fattened calf because he is back safe and sound." He became angry, and when he refused to enter the house, his father came out and pleaded with him. He said to his father in reply, "Look, all these years I served your orders; yet you never gave me even a young goat to feast on with my friends. But when your son returns who swallowed up your property with prostitutes, for him you slaughter the fattened calf." He said to him, "My son, you are here with me always; everything I have is yours. But now, we must celebrate and rejoice, because your brother was dead and has come to life again; he was lost and has been found."

Page 81, Matthew 5:1–12, The Sermon on the Mount

When he saw the crowds, he went up the mountain and after he had sat down, his disciples came to him. He began to teach them, saying:

Blessed are the poor in spirit, for theirs is the kingdom of heaven.

Blessed are they who mourn, for they will be comforted.

Blessed are the meek, for they will inherit the land.

Blessed are they who hunger and thirst for righteousness, for they will be satisfied.

Blessed are the merciful, for they will be shown mercy.

Blessed are the clean of heart, for they will see God.

Blessed are the peacemakers, for they will be called children of God.

Blessed are they who are persecuted for the sake of righteousness, for theirs in the kingdom of heaven.

Blessed are you when they insult you and utter every kind of evil against you (falsely) because of me. Rejoice and be glad, for your reward will be great in heaven. Thus they persecuted the prophets who were before you.

AFTERWORD

The Old and New Testaments present a formidable challenge for any reader even when taken separately. Some may feel unable—even unwilling—to grasp the full import of scripture and its message for their daily lives. How many times has each of us found Bible verses and stories too long or overly complicated to understand? When that happens, The Book is returned to the shelf, resting there as a silent witness to missed opportunity for untold graces and inspiration.

You have now seen and felt what Greg Hadley has done for those who seek a deeper relationship with their God through scripture. He has taken small passages and shared with you his own struggles and victories in life based on sacred scripture. With extraordinary candor, he explains how certain passages have come alive for him with insights and meaning for daily living. The most avid lover of the Word of God has found fresh interpretation and practical application in Greg's writing. His simple language takes each selected verse and story and fills it with contemporaneous relevance. He provides a model anyone can easily follow to find food for the soul.

Thank you, Greg, for sharing this labor of love with us.

Sr. Joan Hansen, SNJM
Lake Oswego, OR

ABOUT THE AUTHOR

Greg Hadley moved from Minnesota to California in 1952 to attend the University of San Francisco. He later attended the MBA executive education program at Pepperdine University and the Owner/President Management Program at the Harvard Business School, Cambridge, Massachusetts. He and his wife, Evelyn, now reside in Lake Oswego, Oregon.

Greg spent his professional life in the business world. He worked for IBM and was General Manager of Computer Sciences of Australia. In 1970, Greg and his associates began acquiring manufacturing businesses and various real estate holdings. During a twenty-year period, Hadley and his partners bought, operated, and eventually sold most of the companies. Since moving to Oregon in 1990, Greg has developed a management consulting practice serving 140 Pacific Northwest companies. He has also been a guest lecturer at the Stanford Graduate School of Business, and has served as an adjunct lecturer in finance at the University of Oregon MBA program. Greg remains active in civic affairs and is a sought-after public speaker.

Greg spent thirty-nine years as an amateur baseball umpire, mostly at the NCAA Division 1 level. He has also been active in his parishes throughout his adult life, and was especially involved in the Rite of Christian Initiation of Adults. He is the author of three previous books. The first, *Fundamentals of Baseball Umpiring* (Perfection Form Company, 1981), is displayed at the National Baseball Hall of Fame in Cooperstown, NY. His second, *Common Problems; Common Sense Solutions* (iUniverse, 2004), is directed to the operators of small to midsized companies. The third, *100 Everyday Epiphanies—Simple Events That Can Inspire Prayer* (Wine Press Publications, 2005), is an acclaimed prayer book. For details, e-mail greg@gbhadley.com.

GREG HADLEY

Made in the USA